CICERO THE PATRIOT

By

Rose Williams

"I think you ought to know what I have accomplished."
Magni mea interesse putarem et res eas quas gessissem tibi notas esse.

– Marcus Cicero Imperator
Salutem Dicit Catoni, *Epistulae*, Book 15, Letter 4

Bolchazy-Carducci Publishers, Inc.
Wauconda, Illinois USA

Editor
LeaAnn A. Osburn

Cover Design & Typography
Adam Phillip Velez

Cover Illustration and p. 25
John Leech for Gilbert à Beckett,
Comic History of Rome (London, 1852);
(reprint 1996 by Bolchazy-Carducci Publishers, Inc.) p. 291

Cicero the Patriot

Rose Williams

Bolchazy-Carducci Publishers, Inc.
1000 Brown Street
Wauconda, IL 60084 USA
www.bolchazy.com

Printed in the United States of America
2004
by United Graphics

ISBN 0-86516-587-4

Library of Congress Cataloging-in-Publication Data

Williams, Rose, 1937-
  Cicero the patriot / by Rose Williams.-- 1st ed.
    p. cm.
  ISBN 0-86516-587-4 (pbk. : alk. paper)
  1. Cicero, Marcus Tullius. 2. Statesmen--Rome--Biography. 3. Orators--Rome--
Biography. 4. Rome--Politics and government--265-30 B.C. I. Title.

  DG260.C5W55 2004
  937'.05'092--dc22

                                                    2004019770

CONTENTS

INTRODUCTION

Illum ipsum consulatum suum non sine causa,
sed sine fine laudabat.

He praised his own achievements not without cause
but without end.

Seneca Minor, *Dialogorum*, X,5.1 *(De Brevitate Vitae)*

Marcus Tullius Cicero had his share of human frailties. He combined great natural ability and hard work with a very high opinion of his own worth. He truly loved his country and took great risks for it, but he always thought his efforts could have been appreciated much more than he felt they ever were. Republican Rome was one of those annoying societies profusely provided with offshoots of great family trees, some in a bad state of decay but still affording their offspring a boundless sense of superiority, even in the face of their personal total worthlessness. A man such as Cicero, keenly aware of his personal gifts and the contributions he had made to his society by those gifts, did not appreciate being sneered at by some chinless wonder of the aristocracy. It is not surprising that he trumpeted his own successes; he felt that somebody needed to, and shyness was never one of his faults.

When young, Cicero honed his remarkable speaking skills under the tutelage of two great actors—Roscius the comedian and Aesopus the tragedian. There was something uncannily prognostic in this, as he became in a small sense a comic, and in a large sense a tragic, figure. With Roscius he polished his acerbic wit and his appreciation of the ironic, and his insistence upon blaring forth his own good qualities gave him a humorous aspect that the suave, assured Caesar and the bluff warrior Pompey both escaped. His life, however, was essentially a tragedy. His very deepest love was given to two objects—the Roman Republic and his daughter Tullia, and in the end he lost them both. His words to Antony in the *Second Phillipic* are eerily prophetic: "I defended the Republic as a young man; I shall not desert her now that I am old; I despised the swords of Catiline, I shall not fear yours. Indeed I would offer this body gladly, if in dying I might leave the Roman people free." *(Second Philippic Oration on Mark Antony)* The irony is that this brave but foolhardy statement and the gruesome death it brought on him ultimately helped free the country from Antony's power, but neither this nor anything else could salvage a Roman Republic which was definitely on its last legs.

CHAPTER I
A STAR IS BORN

Quid enim est aetas hominis, nisi ea memoria rerum
veterum cum superiorum aetate contexitur?

For what is human life, unless it is interwoven with the life of
our ancestors by the records of history?

Orator, 120

One of the greatest of the Roman patriots, in the eyes of the world as well as in his own, was born in the little town of Arpinum on January 3, 106 BC. It is doubtful that Marcus Tullius Cicero would have approved of such a run-of-the-mill birthplace; he would probably have preferred to be born in the Roman Curia (senate house), or perhaps on the *rostra** in front of it. Fortunately for his mother, he had no say in the matter. He would find one connection with his birthplace to boast of, however (not counting those endless diatribes on the joys of country life that he, like other Roman city slickers, so often indulged in). When Cicero was born, another citizen of Arpinum, Gaius Marius, had just completed the first of his seven consulships and was drawing a bead on his second. Marius, like Cicero, came from an equestrian family. The equestrian class in Rome were usually wealthy (the very term "equestrian" comes from the Latin word *equus,* which means "horse," and seems in the beginning to have indicated that a man so designated had enough money to buy one of those four-footed passes of admission to the cavalry). Of the social classes of Rome this was Next to the Top, or Second Best, and nothing gives people the heebie-jeebies like being Second Best. Bottom of the Barrel folk, who among Roman citizens were called plebeians, often just shrug it off and scrape along as best they may, hoping to keep the bills paid and the wolf from the door. Second Best folk, on the other hand, are antsy. They often feel that in a better-organized world they would be Top of the Heap, and they set about reorganizing the existing world. Second Best Folk with money are very prone to set about using that money to move up to their Rightful Place in Society.

Marius had not had the money, but he had had plenty of ambition and a powerful patron,* one of the great Metelli clan. (The Metelli were patricians, or Top of the Heap. This class took its name from *pater,* the Latin word for "father," which also meant "Senator." According to Roman legendary history, the first king, Romulus,* had chosen one hundred of these to advise him, and they had advised him right into an early death during a thunderstorm, after which they had piously declared him a god. Their descendants kept a strong hold on positions of power and anything else desirable they could get their little mitts on.) Getting his start by Metellus' recommendation, Marius' military skill had gained him elected office, which brought a seat in the Senate* and therefore patrician standing, even if he bore the far from flattering title of *novus homo,** or new man to Roman politics, when he was elected consul. He had crowned his success by marrying Julia, the aunt of Julius Caesar, and allying his blood with some of the bluest in Rome.

The Cicero family had money, an older equestrian standing than the Marii, and the success of Marius, who was a distant relative, as an example. When Cicero *Pater* discovered that his eldest son showed signs of being a prodigy, or at least an "A" student, he bought a house in Rome so that young Marcus and his brother Quintus might have a Proper Education befitting future leaders of the Roman Republic, including intensive training in philosophy and rhetoric, aimed at making first rate speechmakers of the boys, and the military training necessary for the general tenor of life in Rome. (The Ladder of Success

---

* Words and phrases marked with an asterisk are explained in more depth in Appendix One.

in ancient Rome had two sections—military service and political office. Whereas Marius had been a wonder in the first section and had made quite a mess of the second, Marcus Cicero was destined to be no great shakes as a soldier but an incredible politician. Since Rome was not often lucky enough to get both articles in one package, she had to make do with what she got, sometimes to everybody's disadvantage.)

Cicero, who combined great native ability with a monstrous passion for work, was such an outstanding student that fathers of his schoolmates would often visit the school to observe him in action and see if his quickness in learning that the other boys had reported really existed. (The boys may well have regretted opening their big mouths when their papas started asking why they didn't do as well.) He loved every kind of learning but was particularly fond of poetry and wrote quite a bit of it as a youngster. (The largest surviving specimen, however, which was written in his adulthood, doesn't give Vergil, Horace and Ovid much to worry about. It might have more of a following today if it did not begin with the line *"O fortunatam natam me consule Romam!"* (Cf. "Cicero's Poetry,"* p. 80). This little gem didn't do much for Cicero's reputation for humility, which wasn't outstanding to start with.

CHAPTER II
POLISHING THE GEM

Nihil in hominum genere rarius perfecto
oratore inveniri potest.

Nothing rarer can be found in the race of man
than an accomplished orator.

De Oratore, I, 128

As his education advanced, Cicero studied under Diodotus the Stoic* and Philo the Academic,* learning logic from the first and eloquence from the second. His attachment to poetry encouraged him to polish his literary efforts; it also led him to seek the company and conversation of such men as Archias the Greek poet and the aged Roman dramatist Accius. (No doubt this is better than seeking the company of gamblers and ladies with shady reputations, but it does make a boy seem a bit dull and lessen his chances for a Biography series.) Listening to the great speakers in the Roman Forum both taught him good speechmaking and fired his ambition. He boasted that no day passed that he did not practice oratory (*De Claris Oratoribus*, 309). Although this habit may have led to a sad shrinking of his pool of boon companions, it was great training for his future.

Never a dim-witted youngster, he quickly noted that the excellent speeches in the Forum could have benefited from more grace and less wood in their delivery. He studied effective gestures, etc., from Roscius the comic actor and Aesopus, a tragedian. (This was eminently sensible of him, since politicians are frequently consciously or unconsciously comedians, and, if their policies have much effect, quite often become tragedies, if not outright disasters.) His education received further polish from extensive studies in Greece (where every well-to-do Roman youngster who possessed ambitions, or a father who cherished ambitions, went to Finishing School), in company with his brother Quintus and a pair of first cousins. Also receiving education with Marcus and Quintus were several friends, one of whom, Titus Pomponius, would be Marcus' confidant and comforter throughout his life.

This Titus Pomponius, who as we shall see earned for himself the nickname Atticus, was an amazing person. His father was a wealthy equestrian who was greatly interested in literature and was bent on a fine education for his son. As a boy, Titus, like his friend Marcus Cicero, had a natural capacity for learning. He also had a very agreeable manner and tone, in lamentable contrast to his friend. People of every walk of life might admire Cicero, but his dedication to telling the truth as he saw it, and his swift and acerbic tongue in doing so, often made enemies. (People find it hard to forgive somebody who makes telling remarks that they have a sneaking suspicion may be insights into the unvarnished truth. Most people prefer their truth with as much varnish as possible.) Titus Atticus, who was evidently very good at applying a smooth finishing coat to his remarks, from his youth up was a friend to everybody. Scholars may scoff at his unflagging amiability and friendship with absolutely everybody as "prudent mediocrity" if they choose; in the Rome of his day it was a mind-boggling achievement. No one else seems to have managed it; of course, it isn't on record that anyone else tried.

Titus' father died when he was quite young, and, taking stock of his situation, the young man observed that Cornelius Sulla on the patrician side and a politician named Cinna on the plebeian side were making Rome a perfect Hades for each other's adherents. Titus was related by marriage to a plebeian tribune named Publius Sulpicius who had just met a gruesome end, and it was obvious that the chancy game of Choosing a Side was becoming necessary in Rome and that one had a fifty-fifty chance of making the wrong choice and winding up on the rapidly increasing list of the dear departed. Having at best a tepid interest in politics and a very lively interest in keeping his head in close association with his shoulders, Titus decided that this was an excellent time to move, lock, stock and financial assets, to Athens, where he made himself very useful to, and consequently very beloved by both the Athenians and whatever displaced Romans came to him for help. Nepos records that Titus' aptitude for getting along with everyone resulted in his becoming even richer than his father had left him, as he inherited the vast wealth of his maternal uncle Quintus Caecilius, with whom Pomponius alone of all humanity could remain on amicable terms.

Marcus Cicero's volatile younger brother Quintus married Titus' sister Pomponia, only to discover that Titus, the greedy rascal, had evidently made off with all the agreeable nature to be had in the Pomponian clan. At least there was absolutely no evidence that his sister had any of it. Quintus himself was a bit on the testy side. (Marcus always said that his little brother was "sensitive," an overworked word which anxious relatives often use to describe a person who is constantly affronted by something somebody did or did not do or say.) The result of all this was a merry marriage for which either Marcus or Titus or both often did referee duty. (Many of Cicero's letters written to Titus through the years indicate both their efforts in this area— sometimes these efforts were fruitful, sometimes not.)

Back in Rome, Cicero studied law under the Mucii Scaevolae, great statesmen and leaders in the senate descended from one of the earliest Republican heroes. (This was Caius Mucius Scaevola,* or Lefty, without whom the Roman Republic might have died a-borning.) Cicero gained from them knowledge of the Roman laws, which were quite extensive and involved, and a feeling that any Roman worth his salt should be doing something for the Old Republic.

Next it was time for a little military service, which Cicero hoped would be as little as possible. Beginning in the year 90 BC, he served a short time in the Social War under Gnaeus Pompeius Strabo, the father of Pompey the Great, and to his horror found himself for a short time under the command of Lucius Cornelius Sulla, who had superintended the demise of his rival Cinna and was now drawing a bead on Marius. Sulla had nice blue Roman blood, a factor that never hurt a Roman politician even if, as in Sulla's case, that blue blood had been largely on holiday from public service for a few centuries. Sulla was steadily moving forward to make himself dictator,* which goal he achieved in 84 BC. As was mentioned earlier, Cicero's friend Titus

Pomponius, who was very sure that he wanted no part in the looming nasty events, in 85 BC had taken himself and his immense wealth to Athens in Attica, where he stayed for the next twenty years. This bit of eminent good sense earned him the title of Atticus. In Athens he led a quiet life of cultured refinement and good works augmented by sharp business skills, and, with an unmatched talent for survival, managed to avoid politics completely. He gave every possible aid and comfort to Cicero, but he also helped all prominent politicians of every stripe, when they were in need, from Marius to the young Octavian Caesar, soon to be named Augustus.

CHAPTER III
MAKING A NAME

Cedant arma togae, concedat laurea linguae

Let arms yield to the toga; let the victor's laurel yield
to the orator's tongue

De Consulato Suo

Cicero delivered his first speech, the *Pro Quinctio*, in 81 BC. While a respectable performance, this little effort didn't exactly set the world on fire; that was accomplished by his second speech, the *Pro Roscio Amerino*, in the following year. Chrysogonus, a freedman who was one of the Dictator Sulla's less engaging boon companions, had a wealthy man named Sextus Roscius killed and inserted his name in Roscius' will. When the defrauded son of Roscius found himself accused of patricide and set out to find a lawyer willing to take his case against Sulla's henchman, he found a marked lack of enthusiasm in the practitioners of the legal profession. Cicero, however, with the youthful, courageous, honest fervor that marked him throughout his career (and had its part in bringing that career to an abrupt end) took on the defense of young Roscius, and succeeded so well that there was an acquittal. The whole plot was revealed and Cicero's fame was established.

Cicero, like Lord Byron, woke to find himself famous, but at the cost of exposing some of the seamy underside of Sulla's reign and the nasty nature of some of his closest associates. Although Cicero wisely took the position that Sulla was unaware of these dastardly deeds, after young Roscius was acquitted, he felt it was best to go to Greece for the sake of his health. Exactly what kind of threat his health faced he carefully left unspecified. He spent the next two years traveling and studying in Greece. Upon the news of Sulla's death in 78 BC, however, his gloomy view of his health and longevity chances underwent an amazing change, and he soon sailed for home.

In 77 BC Cicero became engaged to Terentia, a wealthy woman who could boast of a patrician heritage, being related to the great Fabii who had long made a habit of making Rome's enemies wish they had picked on somebody else. He led her into matrimony, as the Latin idiom goes, but according to Plutarch that was the last time he was allowed to take the lead. He quotes Cicero as saying that she preferred to thrust herself into his public affairs rather than approaching him with her dissatisfactions, and credits her in later years with driving Cicero through her violent temper and jealousy into a testimony against Clodius the Gorgeous which put our orator in very hot water. (Plutarch always knew more than he should have about private matters, and one wonders where he got his information. As he wrote one hundred years after Cicero died, it seems unlikely that he bribed the housemaids. Maybe he rummaged around among Cicero's private letters, which the ever-helpful secretary Tiro published after Cicero's death.)

About the time of his marriage Cicero gave another outstanding speech, the *Pro Roscio Comoedo.* This defendant is not to be confused with young Roscius of Ameria whom he had previously defended against the charge of patricide. This prisoner at the bar was his actor friend, and the case concerned damages paid for the death of a slave pupil. (Now therein lies a tale, only none of our sources seems to want to tell us what it is.)

In 76 BC his life was brightened by the birth of his daughter Tullia, whose company would always be his greatest joy. In one of his letters to his brother Quintus, Cicero remarked that she was affectionate, unassuming, and talented—the very replica of her father (*Ad Quintum Fratrem* I.3).

In Cicero's varied and dangerous life among some of the most fascinating (and deadly) people who ever lived, the lively Tullia and the wise and stable Atticus would be the shining lights in the murky darkness that was always waiting to swoop down on him.

Now it was time for elected office, if Cicero was ever to get where he wanted to go, which was to the top of the Roman political ladder. One did this by moving through the *cursus honorum*,* a series of elective Roman magistracies. In 75 BC Cicero was elected quaestor,* (first rung of this political ladder), for Western Sicily, whose inhabitants got a refreshing surprise from his just government, and learned to love him for his kindly and humorous nature. They were so complimentary that he was sure everyone in Rome was singing his praises. Unfortunately, when he arrived at the Bay of Naples on the way home, he met an important Roman whom he considered a friend and asked him what the Romans had said and thought of his recent achievements. His friend startled him by asking, "Now where have you been, Cicero?" In later years he made an amusing anecdote of this blighting experience, but it is doubtful that it afforded him much amusement at the time. It did teach him, however, that the motto of the Roman people (or any other people for that matter) was likely to be "out of sight, out of mind." After this he stayed as close as he could to the capital city itself, and saw to it that his activities did not go unheralded, even if he had to do the heralding himself.

CHAPTER IV
GETTING TO THE TOP

Nihil tam munitum quod non expugnari pecunia possit.
No place is so strongly fortified that money cannot capture it.
In Verrem, I, 2, 4

His just reward for his good treatment of the Sicilians was coming, however, in the case of the despicable Roman governor Verres. In 70 BC, when Cicero was aedile-elect, the Sicilians brought prosecution against Verres for extortion. Even for a Roman governor Verres was a first-class rotter, but he was not a stupid rotter, and he well knew that prosecution was coming. Therefore he set out to stack the deck. (The Romans had their share, perhaps more than their share, of greedy, unscrupulous, and cruel people. Woven in among these, however, was a sizeable number of rigid moralists who wrote fair rules and could get decidedly unpleasant with anyone who broke these rules. So, if a man wanted to be one of those incredibly nasty Romans whom both stage and screen love so dearly, he had better prepare a safeguard against the retribution sure to be aimed at him by the rigid moralists.) Verres' safeguard was the collection of three fortunes. One, he said, was for himself, the second for his lawyer, and the third for his jury. He selected Hortensius, the foremost lawyer in Rome and consul-elect for the coming year, to be his advocate. (Of course Hortensius should have had nothing to do with such an unsavory affair, but, like so many lawyers ancient and modern, he was fully imbued with that "innocent until proven guilty" notion.)

The Sicilians promptly employed Cicero to represent them. Verres then tried to get himself a bit of insurance by finagling so that a certain Caecilius instead of Cicero should prosecute him and the whole thing would be a sham. Cicero first had to file suit to get himself declared the Sicilian's rightful representative. He won that round and was granted one hundred and ten days in which to visit Sicily and collect evidence.

Verres was not bested yet. He now hoped to postpone his trial until after the first of the year, when Hortensius would be consul. (The Romans evidently didn't give a lot of thought to conflict of interest.) Verres set up the prosecution of the recently returned governor of Achaia for extortion and got the case entered in the court of the praetor* ahead of his. This lawyer also had one hundred and ten days to gather evidence, and should have reported two days before Cicero.

Verres, who obviously did not know any of Cicero's old schoolmates and had no idea what a dynamo he was dealing with, got an unwelcome surprise when Cicero returned after only fifty days with masses of evidence and numbers of witnesses—he had enough material to prosecute half a dozen governors. Verres may well have wished he had not been quite so thorough in his greed, especially in a province friendly to Cicero.

The trial was set for August 5, 70 BC. From August 1 until January 1, the calendar of Rome was one long series of holidays. (The Romans, having no weeks, had no weekends. They made up for this by taking their weekend breaks all in a row.) Therefore, Verres and Hortensius could have dragged an ordinary trial out until the year of Hortensius' consulship, but they soon discovered that, with Cicero as prosecutor, this was unlikely to be an ordinary trial. Rather than droning on for several days, as was the custom, outlining his case and then sitting through Hortensius' rebuttal, Cicero went right to the evidence, which was damning—so damning that Hortensius threw out Verres and his case, and Verres went into exile. Cicero, who had reluctantly passed up a chance to make a brilliant speech, then published it to show everybody what they had missed since Verres had been too cowardly to stay around for the trial. After this masterful display, Cicero was the established head of the Roman bar, and Hortensius ceded to him the most honored place in speaking. (As famous orators, like other public figures, are likely to possess large and tender egos, we might suspect that Hortensius did not do this easily, or without developing a major case of indigestion. According to Nepos, Atticus' biographer, Atticus "achieved the very difficult feat of preventing conflict between two men who so competed for glory." Atticus with all the amazing persistence, prudence, and grace which Cicero often praised in him, was well embarked on his career of reconciling the irreconcilable.)

Cicero, remembering the Roman populace's "out of sight, out of mind" attitude, signed his father's house over to his brother and lived near the Palatine in order to be handy for those who wanted to show up for his morning *salutatio**—that early dawn ritual in which clients,* dependents, and those down on their luck visited the homes of influential men looking for one kind of handout or another. Plutarch insists that Cicero's morning gathering had just as many visitors as came to the two Big Men in Rome of the time: the immensely rich Crassus, and Pompey the powerful general.

CHAPTER V
UP THROUGH THE OFFICES

*Nihil est incertius vulgo, nihil obscurius voluntate hominum,
nihil fallacius ratione tota comitiorum.*

Nothing is more unreliable than the populace, nothing more
obscure than the intentions of men, nothing more deceptive than
the whole electoral system.

Pro Murena, 36

While all this was going on, Cicero had been elected aedile,* the second step in his political career, for the year
69 BC. This office was not strictly speaking part of the
cursus honorum, but it was useful for making a name for oneself, as
aediles cared for roads and religious affairs, distributed the food-
stuffs, and entertained the Roman populace with expensive games.
Ever since the Second Punic War, when Hannibal had spent sixteen
years roaring up and down the Italian peninsula scaring the liver out
of the country folk and forcing them to take up residence in town,
Rome had had a large, restless lower class that had better be well entertained—or else. Neither Cicero nor his wife had the kind of money
needed for really mind-boggling games, nor did they have the opportunity to borrow the money as Caesar did. Cicero did have one advantage, however. Even though he was a stickler for the Roman custom
of receiving no fees from those he represented legally (a custom that
would sadly reduce the number of legal practitioners in the modern
world), the grateful Sicilians brought him all kinds of presents. These
he used to reduce the price of grain for the Roman public. Between
this, his careful and fair distribution of said grain, and his readiness
to help people with his legal services, Cicero got through the office
with his head and his popularity in good shape.

The next step on the ladder to success was the office of praetor. As he had for the office of quaestor, he ran for this office at the earliest possible age, and he was elected for the year 66 BC. This election was contested and the votes had to be counted three times, but since each tally showed that Cicero had the most votes, there was nothing much to do but award him the office. Now for the first time he gave a purely political speech, on the great Roman *rostra*, advocating the passage of the Manilian Law, sensibly named for the tribune Manilius, who had introduced it. It proposed Pompey's appointment as supreme commander of the war against Mithradates VI,* the perennially troublesome king of Pontus. The conservative members of the Roman Senate were against this appointment, as they had been earlier against the command given to Pompey over the entire Mediterranean Sea and the coasts fifty miles inland. Pompey, when given that command, had freed the seas of pirates and devastated the pirate strongholds within three months. This feat did not relieve the Senators' fears; in fact, it added to them. Ever since the early Senate had removed the last of the Roman kings, Tarquin the Arrogant (who had lived up to his name with enthusiasm), many Senators had had a marked tendency to froth at the mouth (and worse yet, make interminably long speeches) when confronted with anyone who might be suspected of the remotest desire to make himself a king. *Rex*, or "king," had been promoted at that time to the dismal status of the dirtiest word in the Latin language, and consuls were always elected in pairs and carried on state affairs on alternate days. (While this arrangement tended to keep any one top magistrate from consolidating power, it created some really remarkable complications during wartime.) Almost four and one half centuries had passed since that momentous era, but Senators had long memories. Their attitude had not changed, and Pompey looked like *rex* material to them. Cicero's clever speech, however, drew a vivid picture of the dismal situation in Asia, which King Mithradates was gleefully making more dismal every day, and gave a forceful argument for Pompey's ability to deal with that situation. Since there was abundant evidence that somebody had better deal with Mithradates, and soon, the forceful speech won the day for Manilius' law. It also won the support of the Pompeians for Cicero.

At the close of his praetorship, Cicero was eligible for the governorship of a province. With so many officials elected every year for a single one-year term, the Roman government had an oversupply of ex-magistrates, and took the sensible view that they might as well get some use out of these retired officials' hair-raising experiences. Cicero, however, still remembering the short memories that the Roman populace had for heroes, decided to stay in the capital and make sure everyone knew he was there. In July 65 BC he asked Atticus' help in running for consul,* since he had the giant handicap of being a *novus homo.* Very few men in recent generations had won the consulship if their family tree did not already contain a consul* or two. The most notable exception to this unwritten rule had been Cicero's townsman Marius. One thing in Cicero's favor, however, was the ghastly nature of his chief opponent, Lucius Sergius Catilina.

CHAPTER VI
THE CATILINE AFFAIR

O tempora, o mores! Senatus haec intellegit, consul videt;
hic tamen vivit.

Oh the times, oh the customs! The Senate knows these things,
the consul sees them; yet this man lives.

In Catilinam I, 1

L ucius Sergius Catilina was about two years older than Cicero, and had sprung from an old patrician family which had lost most of its influence, the bulk of its wealth, and all of its honor, if it had ever had any. He had been one of Sulla's least pleasant young friends and had found his prospects drying up after Sulla's demise. Even after doing away with his father-in-law and inserting his brother's name in the proscription list to raise money for his activities, most of which delicacy forbids us to mention, he had found himself short of funds and was always having to borrow. Now as birds of a feather have always had that lamentable tendency to flock together, he had naturally made friends with some very unsavory characters, and on top of this had collected an impressive number of creditors. In spite of these facts he had still managed to get himself elected to office, notably the praetorship. After his praetorship in 68 BC, unlike Cicero, he did not decline a provincial governorship. In 66 BC he went to Africa, where he set new records for cruelty and oppression; so much so that he found, when he wanted to run for consul for the year 65 BC, that he was disqualified by charges of extortion. (During the subsequent trial Cicero said that Catiline would run again in the next year "if the jury decides that the sun does not shine at noon." Evidently it did, as we find Catiline up and running in 64 BC.) The delay was very frustrating for Catiline. He was short of money as usual, and he wanted to serve Rome as he had Africa: by taking over the country and plundering the wealthy (and, considering the clamor of his creditors, the sooner the better). As the *piece de resistance* in Rome he planned to remit all debts, beginning with his own. Of course he did not announce this charming program when he ran for consul, but the senate had a fair idea of what he had in mind. They well knew that Catiline was a thoroughly despicable human being, but also that he had some very dangerous characteristics, such as tireless strength, exceptional intelligence, and a charismatic power of speech that drew followers to him. The possible use to be made of such qualities by a man like Catiline, totally lacking in principle, gave even the more unimaginative patricians nightmares, and sent them searching high and low for a champion, and a smooth-tongued one, if they could find him. Gritting their teeth, the senators supported Cicero, though he was a *novus homo* who had risen from the upstart equestrian class by the power of his tongue.

Catiline had always had some idea of killing the consuls whom he could not replace by election. In 65 BC he had evidently made such a scheme and had been frustrated. This time his patience, which had never been very thick in the first place, ran thin. He made a lot of inflammatory speeches about the downtrodden poor, borrowed a lot of money, hid caches of military supplies in various places, and placed another Sullan leftover, Gaius Manlius, in the hills of Etruria above modern Florence with troops. Meanwhile he stayed in Rome, collecting around himself the malcontents and anarchists with which any large and powerful capital is always all too well supplied, and promising them rich rewards from the looting of Rome. Many impoverished men, demoralized by the long civil strife brought on by Marius and Sulla, swelled the ranks of these far from trustworthy citizens.

Now among his impoverished and demoralized ranks Catiline had enrolled one Quintus Curius, who evidently agreed with the playwright Plautus that a lover with an empty purse won't get far. While he was whispering sweet nothings in the shell-pink ears of a lady named Fulvia and noting a certain coldness in her response, he suddenly began boasting of coming power and wealth and promising her the mountains and the seas. (It is not on record that she had asked for these; she probably had something a little more spendable in mind.) When she showed signs of disbelieving him, he told her far too much about Catiline's plans. She shared these gems with a few friends and ended up leaking the plot to Cicero. Cicero, who as consul would be responsible for both the welfare of Rome and number one on the hit list, most vigorously disapproved of Catiline's schemes.

In the election Cicero was first and Catiline's friend Gaius Antonius Hybrida, who had hoped to share a really profitable consulship with Catiline, was second. Thus Cicero and Antonius would be the consuls for the year 63 BC, while Catiline, who ran a very poor third, was out in the cold. Cicero, who knew all about that shared consular power, made it his first priority to pull Antonius' fangs. Catiline should have remembered that his friends, like himself, were likely to change allegiances if offered enough personal gain. Consuls were of course expected to become provincial governors for the year following their consulships, and Cicero had been allotted the rich province of Macedonia. He promptly promised Antonius this prize province, and Catiline soon found that Antonius was an excellent example of a do-nothing official. (This shifty move of Cicero's may have saved Rome, but it could have been very bad news for Macedonia.)

At this point that thin patience of Catiline's ran out completely. He planned an insurrection against the State on October 27, which was to be crowned on the following day by the murder of his opponents, starting with the consul Cicero. His charming companions would then help his power grab along by setting the city on fire. When Cicero's grapevine brought him this interesting tidbit, he called a meeting of the Senate and outlined the situation. After a two-day debate the Senate passed a *senatus consultum ultimum*. This legal action was always embodied in a real gem of rhetoric: "the consuls should see to it that the state was not harmed." What they could and should do to bring about this desirable end was unspecified; thus it conferred dictatorial power on them.

Meanwhile Catiline was roaming around town wearing his best look of injured innocence, but nobody was much impressed. He offered to place himself in custody of various upstanding citizens, but unfortunately they were all too upstanding to want to take charge of Catiline. On the night of November 6 he called a meeting at the house of Marcus Porcius Laeca, and new, improved plans for the burning of Rome and the murder of Cicero were made. A charming pair, Lucius Vargunteius and Gaius Cornelius, volunteered to attend Cicero's *salutatio* the next morning and greet him, not with warm words, but with cold steel. Cicero's spies could hardly wait for the meeting to adjourn to tell him all about it. As a predictable result, the unsavory visitors to Cicero's *salutatio* were denied entrance, and to Catiline's disgust he soon discovered that Rome was not one consul short.

On November 8, the Senate, including Catiline in his best toga, assembled in the Temple of Jupiter Stator, where Cicero considerably startled it by opening the session in a very unusual manner. Foregoing all the usual formulas, he thundered, "How long will you abuse our patience, Catiline?" before the poor plotter could even adjust his pitiful Mistreated and Misjudged face. In this instance Cicero's fiery rhetoric and oratorical skill received some assistance from the natural indignation aroused when he contemplated the messy end he had so narrowly escaped. The impassioned speech that followed showed Cicero's oratorical powers at their best, but it must have been very trying for Catiline. After a moving picture of a city trembling under undeserved threat and a Senate that could not without danger meet in its own senate house,* Cicero got in a few choice innuendos about where Catiline had been the last few nights and what plans he had made. While Catiline was mentally biting his fingernails waiting for whatever specifics Cicero knew to appear in the speech, the wily consul veered off to lament the degraded modern world as compared to the Grand Old Days of Rome. After this digression he suddenly roared, "To death, Catiline, you should already have been led!" While Catiline was getting his hair back in place and readjusting his composure, Cicero dwelled fondly for a while on a number of patriotic Romans who had done in pernicious citizens in various unpleasant ways. Then he brought up the subject of the *senatus consultum* that he held and what excellent use other, more stout-hearted Romans had made of this power. Next he made a glancing reference to the army in Etruria and said that Catiline was under the careful surveillance of "the eyes and ears of many." (By this time Catiline must have felt that this statement was certainly true. He may have entertained a

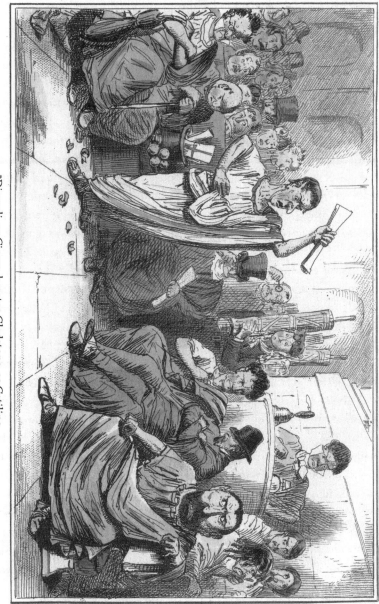

*Disraeli, as Cicero, berates Gladstone, as Catiline.

few wistful thoughts about those old Egyptian rulers who cut out the tongues of people entrusted with their secrets.

Cicero continued to mix nostalgic comments on the extremely permanent punishments visited on Roman traitors of yore with a few concrete facts about that meeting at Laeca's house, wandering off once in a while to insert some uncomplimentary remarks about Catiline's personal habits and way of life. About midway through the speech Cicero mentioned that the seats near Catiline had all been vacated by his fellow senators and, apostrophizing him as an intestinal disease of the state, said that the country was pleading with him to make himself scarce. He ended a really masterly indictment with a pious plea to Jupiter (whose giant statue was conveniently looming behind the speaker) to protect the Roman state and annihilate her enemies.

Catiline tried to counter this powerful and well-documented attack with an appeal to the Senate's well-known snobbery, saying that Rome could not need the protection of an outsider such as Cicero against one of her own patrician sons. Finding that his audience was not buying, he snarled a threat and left town, before anyone should decide to emulate all those pious citizens Cicero had dwelt on so lovingly—the ones who had assassinated their traitorous countrymen. After all, he had depended heavily for his insurrection's success on the Element of Surprise, which is rather hard to maintain after some big-mouthed consul has spilled your plans in a major assembly.

The speech discussed above is known as the *First Oration against Catiline*, so its title gives the wary student due warning that there were more. The *Second Oration*, that was delivered to the people on the next day, celebrated the departure of Catiline and did its noisy best to reassure the populace and scare the hair off the remaining conspirators at the same time. Evidently it went some way toward achieving the latter, and its results showed why the Catilinarian Conspiracy was sure to stub its toe when deprived of its master-mind, Catiline. Some envoys from the Gallic tribe of the Allobroges, who had come to complain about one of those ubiquitous rapacious Roman governors, were in Rome. Cicero had to take some time off to deliver his oration *Pro Murena*, which defended his successor-elect Murena against a charge of bribery. (This speech also became very witty at the expense of Cato, who, like his celebrated ancestor Cato the Censor, was the Archconservative and Perpetual Chairman of Rome's Rigid Moralists). While Cicero was so engaged, the conspirators, feeling somewhat at sea without Catiline's fertile mind, approached the Allobroges hoping for aid. The Allobroges, like the Sicilians some years before, consulted a Roman they felt they could trust, in this case a man by the name of Quintus Fabius Sanga, who was their patron. He told Cicero all about it, and Cicero sent word that the Allobroges should pretend to cooperate with the conspirators still in Rome, who were under the questionable leadership of a gentleman (using the word loosely) with the tongue-twisting name of Publius Cornelius Lentulus Sura. Cicero said that the Allobroges should ask for the conspiracy plans in writing so they could take them back to show to their people. With a naiveté incredible in doughty plotters for government overthrow, Lentulus and company obligingly provided the requested documents complete in devastating detail. The Allobroges, having duly alerted their patron, started home, documents in hand, on the night of December 2. They showed a really touching surprise when arrested at the Mulvian Bridge, and gleefully sent the evidence off to Cicero. On December 3, the Roman Senate assembled again, this time in the Temple of Concord at the base of the Capitoline Hill, to view the evidence and to hear the *Third Oration Against Catiline.*

The predictable result of this coup was that the conspirators found themselves arrested, and the next question was what to do with them. The evidence presented against them was damning, and even people who had thought that Catiline had had a point about remitting the debts were enraged by the plans to burn the city and to involve Gauls in its destruction. The five major leaders of the conspiracy incriminated by the fatal documents were placed in the guardianship of prominent citizens, but the situation was still dangerous. Lentulus in particular was a problem. He was a louse, but a patrician and well-connected louse, and one of those charismatic individuals who make thoughtful people wonder about the wisdom of entrusting a great state to the rulership of the People's Choice. The fact that he had disgraced himself in each successive office had never hindered his election as quaestor, praetor, and consul. The year after his consulship he had been expelled from the Roman Senate by the censors.* (These two top-of-the-trees officials, who outranked even the consuls, were elected every five years for a period of eighteen months, in which they were to count the people for tax purposes and throw out anybody whose morals seemed to call for expulsion). However, the opinion of the censors did not change Lentulus' popularity with the people (especially those on his long payroll), and he had managed to get himself elected praetor for this momentous year in which he was taking part in the Catilinarian conspiracy. He had many unscrupulous followers and dependents who would be not be slow in plotting to rescue him, and Cicero feared they might well succeed, in which case the situation would be one that intelligent people would prefer not to contemplate.

So two days later it was back to the Temple of Concord for the Senate, to discuss what to do with the conspirators. The best and most permanent way to remove the threat of Cethegus, Gabinius, Statilius, Ceparius, and especially Lentulus, would be to execute them, but there were problems with this simple practical solution. Roman law plainly stated that no Roman citizen could be scourged or killed without a trial, and that every indicted Roman had the right to appeal to the people. A long, drawn-out trial could give Lentulus' many dependents time to mount an attack to free him, and giving him the opportunity to appeal to the people might bring on real disaster. To balance against this worrisome law giving Roman citizens the right of trial, Cicero had the *senatus consultum,* which came before all other laws when granted to the consuls to protect the state.

Senatorial discussions, whether about dull matters of routine business or crises likely to destroy the state, followed very strict guidelines, so the first person who spoke in the meeting was the consul-elect Decimus Junius Silanus. This worthy passed up the chance for a long speech and simply advocated the death penalty. Those following him agreed until Julius Caesar, then praetor-elect, brought up the dangers of going against the constitution* by executing citizens in defiance of their rights. Once they began arbitrarily executing Roman citizens, he argued, who could tell where it would end? (Considering what happened to him, Cicero, and others too numerous to mention, he probably had a point). After a few rhetorical arguments with himself, he proposed life imprisonment in Italian towns and confiscation of property. The senators following Caesar agreed with him, partially because of the danger Cicero would face if he executed citizens in so unconstitutional a fashion. Cicero then gave the *Fourth Oration against Catiline*. Insisting that the Senate should consider only the danger to the state, not any danger he might face, Cicero compared the proposals of Silenus and Caesar, tried not to lean too hard on the merits of that of Silanus, and promised to carry out whatever they voted for. The Senate wavered a while, and Tiberius Nero had already proposed an adjournment when a new corner was heard from.

This new corner was young Marcus Porcius Cato, worthy scion of the leading family of those rigid moralists mentioned earlier (and the butt of Cicero's witticisms in the *Pro Murena*). He began his fiery speech by castigating the senators for being more interested in their personal possessions and pleasures than in the *res publica*, and recommended that the Senate do their duty to their country for a change and execute the conspirators before they murdered the Senate and everybody else. After all, he said, the Senators might find it difficult to correct a bad decision after they were dead. This last bit of logic was indisputable, and galvanized the Senate to action. Cato's impassioned speech had definitely decided the issue. The conspirators were executed the next day.

Catiline, learning of the execution of the five conspirators, had a sinking feeling that his little project was definitely a losing proposition. Considering his extremely limited options, he tried to escape into Cisalpine Gaul, but found himself facing a Roman army that was less than kindly disposed toward him. Rightly divining their mood, he fought in a frenzied manner (which was understandable—if anyone ever had reason for a bit of frenzy, it was Catiline at this decidedly unpromising stage of his career). Early in 62 BC he fell fighting at the head of his troops as a good Roman general should. Evidence indicates that this was the only act of Catiline that remotely resembled that of a good general, or a good anything else.

CHAPTER VII
THE REWARDS OF VICTORY

*Trahimur omnes studio laudis et optimus quisque maxime
gloria ducitur.*

We are all attracted by praise, and the best men are especially
motivated by glory.

Pro Archia Poeta, 14

Plutarch says that Cicero was always extremely pleased with his own praise, and continued to the very last to be passionately fond of glory. Cicero himself gave many evidences of this, such as the letter written about this time in which he said to Pompey the Great: "I did expect some congratulation in your letter on my achievements, both for the sake of the ties between us and of the Republic. I suppose you left it out because of a fear of hurting someone's feelings" (*Ad Familiares* 5.7).

The city of Rome, however, was not so stingy with the words of praise. Here at last, as 62 BC chugged along picking up steam, Cicero received a full measure of complimentary rhetoric. Delighted, he wrote that unfortunate poem about Rome's birthdate being in his consulate. Some idiot called him a second Romulus, and even hinted that it was more glorious to found the state a second time than the first. (Later historians have sometimes sneered and said that the Catilinarian conspiracy was no big deal, really. But those later historians did not live in a city that Catiline was enthusiastically planning to put to the torch.) All this praise, especially from the nobility he had always idealized, turned Cicero's head completely, and he reacted by buying a huge residence on the Palatine Hill for an incredible amount of money. (This incredible amount of money was three and one half million sesterces. As monetary worth is the most fluid of measures, that doesn't tell us an awful lot today. We can only say that Cicero, like so many of us, subsequently discovered that it was much more than he should have spent.)

In this momentous year he also delivered perhaps the most unusual of all his orations, the *Pro Archia*. This little effort had a special charm, in that it quickly dispensed with the legal maneuverings and ambled off into a discourse on the value of liberal education. The subject of all this eloquence, Aulus Licinius Archias, was a Greek poet, a native of Antioch, who had come to Rome in the train of Lucius Licinius Lucullus when Cicero was a child. The poet had taken the names Aulus and Licinius, the latter as a compliment to the Luculli, when he had registered with the praetor Quintus Metellus Pius under the *Lex Plautia-Papiria* to become a Roman citizen. He had met all the requirements the *Lex* stipulated: 1) enrollment in an allied city (he was a citizen of Heraclea); 2) a residence in Rome; and 3) timely registration with a praetor. But for some reason his name had been left off the record of the censors in 89 BC, the year in which he attained citizenship. (If the senators et al. had been a little naughtier than usual in the recent past, perhaps the censors had been too busy with censorship to pay close attention to the census.) There was no particular gain to be had from giving Archias a bad time and keeping him from becoming a citizen, but, probably as a way of striking a blow at the powerful Luculli, a man by the name of Grattius prosecuted Archias in 62 BC as a false pretender to the rights of a Roman citizen and demanded that he be forced to leave Rome. He made this demand under the *Lex Papia* of 65 BC, a xenophobic little piece of legislation that required the withdrawal of all foreigners from the city. Archias found himself in a shaky position, and turned to Cicero, who had been his pupil and had a great respect and affection for him.

Cicero started off in a manner unusual for him—he credited somebody else with his speaking ability, or at least the encouraging, polishing, and refining of it. Having said that he was indebted to Archias on this score, he made short work of the legal point, contending that Archias was justified by that very law in question, because before coming to Rome he had resided at Heraclea, a confederate city, and had been enrolled as a Heraclean citizen; and in the law it was expressly provided that those who were registered as citizens of any confederate city, if they were residing in Italy at the time the law was passed, and if they themselves reported to the praetor within sixty days, were to be exempt from its operation. Cicero rapidly summarized all this and then made a few complimentary remarks about the intelligence and refinement of all listening to him. He implied that superior creatures such as they were bound to appreciate the rest of his oration, which he proceeded to spend in praising literature, Archias, and those eminent and noble Romans who had had the good sense to appreciate the poet (and, incidentally, Cicero). Archias is believed to have died soon after this trial. After all, he had been born somewhere around 120 BC and had lived a very full life. On his last legs he might have been, but Cicero saw to it that those legs were declared indisputably Roman.

CHAPTER VIII
JUDGMENT DAY

Cave quicquam incipias quod paeniteat postea.
Be careful about starting something you may regret.
Publilius Syrus

As a result of the Catilinarian conspiracy, Cicero had provided his enemies a perfect weapon against him by executing citizens without a trial and then boasting all over town about it, and he soon inspired a most unscrupulous person with a driving desire to use that weapon. Clodius Pulcher, a scion of the ancient house of Appius Claudius, had all the energy, charm, and general craftiness of his ancestors, but absolutely none of their civic spirit. He had dabbled in politics from an early age, making a promising beginning by inciting the troops of his brother-in-law Lucullus (the patron of Archias) to mutiny and continuing on a lively career of using his famous name to win over or to bludgeon Roman leaders, whichever offered a little profit for himself. To make matters worse, he was just naturally a little bundle of fun and enjoyed stirring up tempers and tempests by pranks as hare-brained as they were outrageous.

In December of 62 BC Clodius decided that it would be great sport to disguise himself as a woman and sneak into the festival of the "Bona Dea." This Bona Dea, or Good Goddess, was a deity worshipped exclusively by women, and all men, from slaves to senators, were barred from her official nocturnal ceremony, which was held yearly in the home of the Pontifex Maximus, or chief priest, under the supervision of his wife and the Vestal Virgins. The Pontifex Maximus at this time was Julius Caesar, and, his beloved Cornelia having died, his wife was Sulla's young and featherheaded granddaughter Pompeia.

Clodius was not called "Pulcher" (Gorgeous) for nothing; no doubt he looked charming in his stola. Nevertheless he was discovered in his woman's dress during the festival, and the ladies turned him in amid much shrieking. Those who loved scandal said he could never have gotten in without a little help from his hostess, and wondered just what sort of persuasion he had used on her. In May of the following year Clodius was tried for sacrilege. Caesar, who had divorced Pompeia in the meantime, refused to testify against Clodius, and when questioned about his recent divorce merely said loftily that Caesar's wife must be above suspicion.

Cicero was not so circumspect. Clodius Pulcher insisted he had been out of town when somebody crashed the Bona Dea festival, but Cicero swore in court that he had spoken with Old Gorgeous in Rome on the fatal day. (According to Plutarch, this is the testimony which Terentia, Cicero's wife, nagged Cicero into making through jealousy of Clodius' sister Clodia. This feminine blot on the Claudian escutcheon could have well been called Clodia Pulchra, along with a few less attractive titles. Cicero sometimes visited Clodia, who lived near him and who was visited by many state leaders. Since this lamentable offspring of the great Appii Claudii combined beauty and wit with an unspeakable reputation, however, most wives thought speaking to her through a glass partition was too close contact for their husbands.) Clodius was narrowly acquitted because the wealthy Crassus, a crony of his, bribed some of the jurors. Then this engaging young man went grumbling off into the background to plot revenge on Cicero for destroying his alibi.

While all these stirring events were taking place in Rome, Quintus, Cicero's brother, who had been climbing up the rungs of the *cursus honorum,* having been aedile in 65 and praetor in 62 BC, was governing the province of Asia. Just before he sailed away to take up his governorship, Quintus seems to have accomplished a Herculean feat—he quarreled with Atticus. In December of 61 BC, Cicero, who was in Rome, found himself (by mail) in the middle of a dust-up between Atticus, who was in Epirus, and Quintus, who was in Asia Minor. Both sides found it a bit difficult to present the only fair side of the argument (their own) to a arbitrator back in the old home town, but they did their best. Atticus had written to Cicero and had enclosed some less than loving missives that he had received from Quintus. Cicero replied that he had been aware before Quintus left for his province that Quintus had a grievance (this is not surprising, as evidence indicates that Quintus' grievances were usually perfectly apparent in his demeanor) but that he had had no luck either in discovering exactly what this grievance was or in soothing his brother's ruffled feathers. Cicero exerted his best efforts in the ways he well knew would appeal to Atticus' generous personality. In one letter he agreed with Atticus about Quintus' complaints, saying that a certain letter from him was like "a lion in front, I don't know what behind" (*Ad Atticum* 2.16). (He had borrowed the Greek for the first part of this statement from Homer's description of the Chimaera [*Iliad,* Book VI, line 181]: "Its front part was a lion, its rear a snake's tail, in between a goat.") He obviously felt that the whole quotation would be a harsh judgment on the letter, and perhaps on his brother.

He also took time out from his busy schedule to write several long letters of criticism and advice to said brother. (It must have been very wearing to try to arbitrate a long-distance quarrel in the ancient world, given the long time necessary to send letters around the Mediterranean. In some instances both combatants and mediators must have gotten over their anger, died of old age, or simply decided that the whole affair wasn't worth the effort and expense.)

Some of Cicero's best letters (and certainly some of his longest) were written to Quintus during his various foreign postings. In the letter helpfully known as *Ad Quintum* I.1 (a fifty-pager), Cicero began by discussing the less than welcome news that Quintus has been assigned a third year as governor of Asia. He apologized for not having been able to get a successor for Quintus appointed, but pointed out that the excellent government which Quintus had administered made it hard to come up with a good successor for him. He praised Quintus greatly for not accepting the various bribes offered him and for governing with the interests of the provincial population at heart. He mentioned that a governor's duty went farther than simply exercising honesty; it was also his duty to see that his subordinates also exercised it. After several high-minded pages of excellent advice, he drew himself up and remarked with perfect truth that his discussion had turned into instruction, which really hadn't been his intention. He then continued calmly with a mixture of instruction and praise, saying that the greatest possible happiness of the governed should be the test of a governor's actions. (Some provincials would have found this statement completely inapplicable to many Roman governors.) He continued with a long list of compliments for Quintus' two years of service conducted along such lines, and a lengthy digression on various great men, including Plato, and what they had to say about government. About 40 pages into this *opus,* he got down to the nub—everyone was in agreement that Quintus was the most admirable of mortals until something put him out of temper; then, it can be inferred, his brother could give an excellent imitation of a Fury.* With praiseworthy restraint he said that he did not expect Quintus to change his nature, and then set forth a list of suggestions about how such a change could be brought about. In a later (and thankfully shorter) letter to Quintus, his older brother said that no one had fault to find with Quintus except in his bitter and angry speech. Evidently Cicero's admonitions to Quintus had about as much effect as such admonitions usually do, but he gets high marks for trying.

Meanwhile the Senate, still laboring under the full force of that *rex* complex, was very cool to Pompey, who had put the Mithradates question to rest once and for all and returned to Rome after annexing Syria, settling an uproar in Judea, and laying an excellent foundation for the reorganization of Asia Minor and the East, which he had pacified. He came home with this solid list of achievements (which any modern politician might well envy), and an impartial observer would have said that there was some reason for his belief that he had earned a positive response to his two requests: that his veterans be provided for and that his arrangements for the peace in the East be ratified.

Unfortunately, impartial observers in the Senate were lamentably few. Cato, the Metelli, and some other high-handed and shortsighted senators, who could just picture him with a crown on his head, refused to honor Pompey's requests or his arrangements. He was both dumbfounded and dismayed, but he didn't stay that way long. The disastrous, at least from the Senate's point of view, result of this haughty act was that he went sulking off to Julius Caesar, whose fertile mind, as always, had something to offer.

What it offered was the formation of the so-called First Triumvirate, an informal arrangement whereby Caesar, Crassus, and Pompey got together and virtually ruled Rome. To this hardly legal but highly effective power structure Crassus contributed money (of which he had managed to collect a staggering supply), Pompey, military prowess, and Caesar, brains and political influence. Caesar, who both valued Cicero's integrity and intelligence and wanted to keep Cicero's brilliant head in close association with the rest of his body, invited Cicero to join the First Triumvirate (which would have made it a quattuorvirate, perhaps, and altered the structure and planning for the Second Triumvirate, not to mention adding another jaw-breaking word to a Latin language already well-provided with them). In addition to his concern for Cicero's safety in the face of his challenges to such unscrupulous types as Clodius, Caesar had always admired men of unimpeachable honesty, such as Cicero and Cato, and liked to work with them. Unfortunately, men of unimpeachable honesty tended to look askance at some of Caesar's methods.

Not only did Cicero look askance at Caesar's methods, but, to make matters worse, he was a Romantic, which is the last thing a politician ought to be. He always viewed the Roman Senate in rosy terms, remembering that Cineas, the spokesman of Pyrrhus, had called it "an assembly of kings," reminiscing fondly about the Catones and the Scipiones,* and conveniently forgetting the Catilinae, the Lentuli and the Verres. He saw himself as leader of a grand coalition of the senators and the equites which would lead the Roman Republic to new and greater heights. But this noble idea sprang a leak because Cicero insisted on seeing the Roman Senate, and the equites for that matter, as they had been in the Good Old Days. Far too many Stern Old Romans had been finished off by the various wars and far too many sons of Stern Old Romans had discovered *la dolce vita*. Caesar understood this, for he had few illusions about himself or anybody else. Cicero, on the other hand, was one of those unnerving individuals who build castles in the air and then energetically attempt to force a hapless real society to live in them.

The Triumvirate soon made its power felt. The equites, always deeply involved in commerce and trade, made some pretty outrageous demands in terms of state contracts that the Senate refused even to consider. Cicero tried to mediate and work out a compromise, but neither side was interested, and the Senate suddenly found itself devoid simultaneously of the military strength of Pompey, whom its unwaveringly haughty attitude had driven over to Caesar's side, and of the backing of the wealthy equites. In this decidedly unpromising situation Julius Caesar was elected consul for the year 59 BC. His colleague was a man named Bibulus, who, after unsuccessfully attempting to veto the Agrarian Law by which Caesar proposed to provide land for Pompey's veterans, threw in the towel and stayed home, attempting to influence Caesar's rapid fire movements by watching the skies for omens. This was not very successful, and the year became known as the consulship of "Julius and Caesar."

While Caesar was legalizing Pompey's arrangements in the East, planting new colonies, compelling the publication of Senate transactions, reducing the taxes that the tax collectors could wring out of the people in Asia Minor, and distributing state lands to poor Roman families that had at least three children, Cicero watched in horror. He did not disapprove of the acts themselves, but he shuddered at their unconstitutionality. When the Senate tried frantically to block each of these, Caesar calmly increased that unconstitutionality by turning to the Assembly of the Roman People,* which passed his bills with enthusiasm.

Clodius meanwhile was making himself useful to the Triumvirate with the popular influence he possessed and plotting revenge on Cicero. For this and other reasons, he persuaded Caesar, the Pontifex Maximus, and the Roman Assembly to change his name from Claudius to Clodius, thus giving him the status of plebeian and allowing him to run for plebeian tribune. When he got this office in 58 BC, he made some beautiful speeches about the sanctity (a word he should have blushed to use, except that he didn't know how to blush) of the law, and proposed the re-enactment of an ancient law which said that anyone who executed a Roman citizen without a trial should be banished. It was all too clear what was brewing in Clodius' nasty little mind. Caesar, who had received the governorship of Gaul for his post-consulate assignment, offered to make Cicero one of the *vigintiviri** (another example of a Roman commission simply labeled by the number of people it involved) appointed to carry out his new agrarian legislation, or a lieutenancy under himself in Gaul. (Either of these posts would have both shielded Cicero from Clodius' spite and conveniently hampered Cicero's barbed tongue.) Pompey, who had made all sorts of flowery and specific promises to help Cicero after he had obtained the Eastern power for Pompey with his speech for the Manilian Law, developed a memory failure and did nothing at all for him. Cicero refused Caesar's offers and fled to Macedonia.

CHAPTER IX
PAYING THE PIPER

Cui placet obliviscitur, cui dolet meminit.
A man forgets his joys; he remembers his sufferings.
Pro Murena, 42

With Cicero out of the country, Clodius showed a lamentable lack of concern for that sanctity of law he had been babbling about and got passage of an unconstitutional bill for Cicero's banishment for putting those henchmen of Catiline to death without a trial. Cicero's beautiful house on the Palatine (which probably wasn't paid for yet) was demolished by Clodius' thugs, and they paid a visit to Cicero's villa at Tusculum which also had disastrous results.

Cicero, believing that he was taking the high road and preserving his independence, had refused Caesar's offers of an honorable and safe position. He had left an Italy that Clodius was making exceedingly unhealthy, just as he had left it years before when Sulla's power was a danger to him. Sitting in Greece in 58 BC and making a careful review of his situation at this point, however, produced a mood that was anything but sanguine. Cicero was a regular bundle of contradictions. Although in many ways he was a textbook example of the politician, a breed not much given to self-blame, passing the buck was never one of his specialties. He had the disconcerting (and often depressing) ability to look any *faux pas* of his own straight in the eye and take full responsibility for it. It was in his nature to take the rocky road of what he considered honor and let Hades take the hindmost, but setting out on the high road of honor can be a quixotic thing to do, especially if a man has a family that may suffer. Few of us can bear with ease the thought that we have gotten ourselves and the people we love into extremely hot water with our bad judgment, and Cicero was no exception. He contemplated suicide, which among Romans was an honorable way out of an intolerable situation, but Atticus convinced him that this was no time to employ a permanent solution to a problem that might well prove to be temporary. Cicero said in a letter that he hoped the day would come when he could thank Atticus for this, but it hadn't arrived yet. In May of 58 BC, while in Thessalonica he wrote to Quintus saying that he hoped in his own ruin he had not ruined his brother (*Ad Quintum Fratrem* 1.3). There was some talk of a prosecution of Quintus, but, as he had had absolutely nothing to do with the execution of those lamentable Catilinarians and was a pillar of undisputed, if somewhat hot-headed, integrity, it came to nothing.

In November of 58 BC in a letter to Terentia, Cicero said: "If, as you wrote, I could think this was 'done by fate,' I might bear it more easily; but all these things were brought about by my fault; I who thought that those who envied me loved me, and who would not follow those who sought me" (*Ad Familiares* 14.1). He said everyone was praising her bravery and strength; obviously hardship had forced Terentia to pull herself together and behave with more courage and less childishness—she even wrote several times to express her gratitude for the help of Atticus, although gratitude had not previously been observable as one of her chief characteristics.

All his misfortunes and an overpowering sense of guilt had a dismal effect on Cicero's spirit and contributed to a sad loss of nerve. In his letters during this definitely unheroic period of his life he wished he had died at Rome and begged his friends to seek permission for his return. Atticus, who had been expending much time and effort in protecting Cicero's family (which, after all, was a part of his own) of course responded energetically to this plea.

In August 57 BC, after an exile of a little more than a year, Cicero was allowed to return to Rome. The populace in general and the senators in particular had gotten more than a little tired of all those attacks on the Roman constitution, such as it was, and he received a rousing welcome all along his return route, from Brundisium to the capital city itself. This not only thrilled his glory-loving heart, but also gave him the entirely false hope that he and the Senate could rebuild the Good Old Days.

Once in Rome he had to endure some far from pleasant surprises. His property was in ruins, and as he told Atticus in a letter, in the realm of finances he was seriously embarrassed. After thanking Atticus for the trouble, zeal, and labor he had expended on Cicero's behalf, he explained that indeed he was welcomed to the full force of his old standing and reputation, but that didn't mean that he could be the power he had once been. The power of the Triumvirate was too strong for opposition, and he was forced to confine his speeches to legal cases concerning individuals, not constitutional arguments. This situation was made all too clear while he was preparing a brilliant speech (at least we gather it would have been brilliant, but unfortunately it died a-borning) questioning the legality of Caesar's *Lex Campania* of year 59 BC. The Senate agreed to hear this speech and debate the matter. At this point Pompey, who had not managed matters in Rome very well while Caesar was in Gaul and was setting new records for unpopularity, took himself off to Luca in 56 BC for a conference with Caesar and Crassus. During this political gathering, Brother Quintus, who was now one of Caesar's legates,* was invited to an informal chat with Pompey (who had made more promises to Cicero since his return but now suffered another of those inexplicable memory losses), at which he was quietly informed that, for everybody's safety, Marcus must be muzzled. To Marcus' dismay he discovered that his carefully prepared speech was not to be delivered, that Pompey and Crassus were to be consuls for the following year, and that Caesar's power in Gaul was to be extended for five years. The First Triumvirate's power was not supported by any legal status, however, so these matters had to be carried out through the usual channels. Crassus and Pompey stood for election, and Cicero was tapped to deliver the speech *De Provinciis Consularibus*, which recommended said extension of Caesar's power in Gaul.

As always when confronted with anything involving Julius Caesar, Cicero found himself in a dilemma. Old style Romans, laboring under that *rex* complex which sometimes resembled paranoia, always feared their most able individuals and sometimes brought their careers to an untimely end by one means or another. Cicero admired Caesar, and could not be unmoved by Caesar's respect and regard for him, but he feared both Caesar's brilliance and his impatience with the cumbersome nature of Roman politics. On the other hand, Gaul needed a powerful man in control. When the Romans had defeated and annexed their northern neighbors the Etruscans in the early days of the Republic, they had found that they had exposed themselves to another neighbor on the north, the Gauls, who were just as fierce as the Etruscans and much less civilized. A number of Roman heroes such as Camillus and Marius had become heroes by dealing with some of the more hair-raising manifestations of Gallic power.

Some time later Cicero explained to P. Lentulus in a letter that at this point he had a little conversation with the *Res Publica,** asking, after all he had suffered for her sake, that she give her permission for him to redeem the pledge of good behavior given by his brother and to show gratitude to those, Caesar in particular, who had helped him. (These little chats with his country were favorites with Cicero. In the *First Catilinarian Oration* he included a touching and powerful speech in which the *Res Publica* pleads with Catiline to go out of the city and leave her in peace. As in the earlier Catiline affair, at this crisis his country seemed very conveniently to agree with Cicero on all points.) He went on to assure Lentulus that consistency in opinions had never been considered a merit in national rulers (*Ad Familiares* 1.9). (This view is certainly well supported by modern politics.)

In his speech *De Provinciis Consularibus,* Cicero reminded the Senate that he had refused every honor and office Caesar had ever offered him. He said that he might be an enemy to Caesar, but he wanted to be a friend to the republic, and the republic needed somebody to put the obstreperous Gauls in their place once and for all. He pointed out that Caesar was well on the road to doing this, and should be allowed to continue. With that poetic and very unrealistic attitude toward natural phenomena so common in literary folk, he calmly stated that Nature had built the Alps to protect Rome from the Gauls. "Let the Alps sink!" he shouted, considerably startling the company and waking a few elder statesmen who had fallen into a light doze. "Soon we will no longer need them." As a result of all this fiery rhetoric, combined with the muscle of the Triumvirate, Caesar got his extension. (The records nowhere indicate, however, that the Alps availed themselves of this permission to relax.)

CHAPTER X
GETTING BACK TO BUSINESS

Lucius Cassius ...in causis quaerere solebat, "cui bono" fuisset.

Lucius Cassius in trying cases always asked,
"Who got something out of it?"

Pro Roscio Amerino, 56

During this period our orator also delivered the *De Domo Sua,* directed against Clodius Pulcher, who, after forcing Cicero into exile, had sneakily consecrated a shrine to Liberty on the site of Cicero's demolished Palatine residence in the pious hope that Cicero could never reclaim it or receive damages for its destruction because it was now sacred ground. Added to his personal animosity to Cicero was the deep-seated belief that financial embarrassment would keep Cicero out of politics. In the narrow but decidedly nasty little mind of Clodius, a man with no money for bribes was not likely to accomplish much on the national stage.

To these turbulent times also belongs the *Pro Caelio,* a speech in which Cicero defended his young friend and pupil Caelius against a charge of engaging in public violence, being accessory to a murder, and attempting to poison Clodia. The abuse Cicero heaped upon Clodia in this speech should have gladdened the heart of Terentia. Beginning with a reference to charges against Caelius being "brought by a prostitute," he goes on to call Clodia "the Medea of the Palatine." Certainly this was a comparison rich with suggestion, as Medea was a beautiful seductive witch who murdered her brother, her children, and other various and sundry individuals who got in her way. Cicero went on to say that by taking this case he had no desire to wound a lady who, far from being the enemy of mankind, was known to be the very good friend of them all. (Clodia had evidently contributed to the accusation against Caelius as a form of revenge because Caelius had wearied of her charms. At least, with Cicero's help, he survived association with Clodia, unlike his good friend the poet Catullus, who may have been the only Roman ever to die of love.)

While these various speeches were successful and achieved their aims, Cicero's every effort was now definitely hampered by the all-seeing eye of the Triumvirate. That republican free speech he delighted in, and which had made him famous, found itself hamstrung by the unyielding determination of three very powerful men.

The year 56 BC found Atticus busily supplying to Cicero aid and comfort which ranged from loans to alleviate financial embarrassment to a pair of library slaves to help Tiro's minions preserve and resurrect the parts of Cicero's library that had survived Clodius' delicate attentions. Quintus, serving his country in Sardinia as a legate of Pompey, evidently thought the right to give advice was not limited to older brothers; to his admonitions Cicero replied that toward politicians and enemies (sometimes one and the same) he himself was behaving just as he ought. "I am always," he said, "softer than the lobe of your ear" (*Ad Quintum Fratrem* 2, 15a).

Whatever his political concerns might be, Cicero was inevitably pulled back to family affairs, which were always simmering if not boiling over. In a letter to Quintus (who was probably not too grieved that business in Sardinia kept him out of the heaving bosom of the family) Cicero says that on his round of visits to the various family properties he found Pomponia complaining about Quintus Senior and his nephew Quintus Junior being tactful about the disputes between Pomponia and Terentia. (This use of tact in a family spat was not a distinguishing characteristic of the Cicerones. Perhaps young Quintus had borrowed a leaf from his Uncle Titus' book. Unfortunately he does not appear to have borrowed that particular leaf very often.) Cicero ends his letter with a loving and solicitous admonition to his brother to take care of his health. Whether this referred to an illness Quintus faced, the political situation, or the vicissitudes of life with Pomponia he does not say.

Meanwhile Cicero was attempting to persuade the historian Lucius Lucceius, who was nearing the end of his history of the Italian wars of 90–81 BC, to employ his busy little mind next in undertaking a history including Cicero's exploits. In a remarkable letter totally devoid of any pretense of personal modesty he detailed how he thought this should be done. (He said that his bashfulness, of which we have never seen any evidence, had prevented him from presenting this request face-to-face). First he exhorted Lucceius to get busy on this project at once, as he was very impatient to see it. He then stated that the story of his troubles and the perfidy of other people toward him should come early in the work and perhaps be a separate section, as his tribulations would make fascinating reading for people who had no troubles of their own. (Where he expected to find this class of readers defies our imagination; it probably defied Lucceius' also.) He explained that he hesitated to write his own panegyric, as men in doing so were obliged to soft-pedal their own achievements, whereas Lucceius would be free to praise him to the utmost. He wound up this singular effusion with a request that Lucceius might let him read and perhaps edit the accolade when it was written, and offered to supply notes. To nobody's surprise but Cicero's, Lucceius did not avail himself of this unique opportunity (*Ad Familiares* 5.12).

Having taken time off to attend the opening of the Theater of Pompey,* Cicero more than half wished that he hadn't. He wrote to his good friend Marcus Marius that if Marius was too sick to attend the festivities, he had been fortunate. If, however, he had been well and still had given the spectacle a miss, he was wise as well as fortunate. Cicero then proceeded to give a review of Pompey's plays that would make the most acerbic drama critic green with envy. First on the stage, he said, there came for the sake of their honor those who for the sake of their honor should have left the stage. After excoriating the settings and props, which were lavish, and everything else, which had a hard time getting up to mediocre, he moved on to the gladiatorial combats, which he said were even worse than most exhibitions of a sport that was a very poor form of entertainment to begin with. On the last day of this lamentable effort at amusement, Cicero said, there was a hunt of elephants driven into the arena to be slaughtered. He said the common people eyed the beasts with wonder, and then with pity, as their confusion and doomed condition reminded the people of themselves. He concluded by stating that Marius would have been much better entertained by listening to his slave read aloud, providing said slave was not reading Cicero's orations.

CHAPTER XI
THE LITERARY LIFE

Haec studia adolescentiam acuunt, senectutem oblectant,
secundas res ornant, adversis perfugium ac solacium praebent.

These studies sharpen the young, delight the old,
enrich our prosperity and give refuge and comfort in adversity.

Pro Archia Poeta, 16

As the year 54 BC rolled along, Cicero dealt as best he could with a rather sticky situation that called for fence sitting, and maybe a bit of high-wire walking. Cicero, who had always preferred to stand on *terra firma*, (in as prominent a position as possible) and to shout the truth as he saw it at the top of his lungs, found this trying, but necessary if he wanted to keep head and body incorporated into a single unit. Caesar and Pompey, in the interest of power and self-preservation, held to their uneasy alliance, but one of their strongest ties was the marriage of Caesar's beloved only Julia to Pompey. With absolutely no consideration for her civic duty Julia died in 54 BC, and the disagreements between Caesar and Pompey escalated. Quintus, on the way to Gaul with Caesar, wrote Cicero some very good advice about keeping the good will of Caesar's adherents while not alienating those of Pompey. (They both could have used some of Atticus' genius for endearing himself to all companions.) In reply Cicero promised to mind his p's and q's, or rather Pompeys and Caesars, and to try to stay out of trouble. The word trouble naturally turned his mind to his son and his nephew, and he promised to keep an eye on both, even tutoring young Quintus, if the touchy youngster would allow it. He said that he would have plenty of time for family in "these days of leisure"—apparently an embittered reference to the fact that he had been largely sidelined in politics. He also mentioned that bribery and corruption had grown so bad in the forthcoming elections that the candidates for tribune had been forced to deposit a pledge for good behavior with Cato, one of the extremely rare breed of totally honest political figures. Cicero had the greatest respect for both Cato's character and his forcefulness, but nevertheless did not envy him the job of keeping the elections aboveboard (*Ad Quintum Fratrem* 2.15b).

Also at this time Cicero gave his attention to building projects not only on his own property but also on Quintus'. In September of 54 BC he wrote to Quintus, now in Britain with Caesar, that he had just visited their various properties which were undergoing some of those constant repairs and improvements that real estate has always required, since it is the time-honored custom of buildings in every era and clime to begin to fall apart on the day that they are built. After delineating the various good points of the building programs and the various bad points of the contractors, he mentioned a small villa of Quintus at Laterium. This little home in the country was evidently a bit Spartan, as after viewing it he chuckled: "By Hercules I approve the additions you had decided to make; as the villa stands it looks like a philosopher, doing its best to shame the extravagance of other villas. Your landscape gardener is very industrious though: he has covered everything, both the foundation-wall of the villa and the spaces between the columns of the walk, with so much ivy that those Greek statues look like they have taken up fancy gardening, and are trying to show off the greenery (*Ad Quintum Fratrem* 3.1). He went on to say that he certainly didn't blame Quintus for asking about his son in every letter and said that he would be happy to tutor him, but that Quintus must write to Pomponia, (who evidently was indulging in her favorite sport of being difficult, if not impossible), telling her to take her son and accompany Marcus whenever he left Rome. It seems she was pretending that she needed Quintus' permission to accompany his brother. Since she paid very little attention to Quintus' wishes when she was in the room with him, we are hard pressed to believe that she really felt so strongly about them when he was a thousand miles away.

In spite of a political environment that became daily more threatening, Cicero showed an endearing interest in young people and tried to help them move safely through a perilous political world. Not content with supervising his son and his nephew and giving whatever help he could to young Caelius, he also aided others, such as a young lawyer named C. Trebatius Testa, who was getting his education the hard way in Gaul with Caesar's army. Marcus mentioned in a letter to Quintus that he himself had recommended Trebatius to Caesar. He said that Caesar had, with his usual generosity, done all that Cicero had expected for Trebatius, and, if Trebatius had not done quite all that he expected, neither Quintus nor Caesar could be faulted for that.

About the time Cicero was inspecting his brother's properties Quintus stood in considerable danger of having no further need for property or anything else. In the fall of 54 BC up in Gaul, Caesar distributed his legions under his subordinate commanders into widely separated winter camps. One legion commanded by Labienus was quartered among the Treveri, Cotta and Sabinus had one stationed among the Eburones, and Quintus had the bad luck to be in command of a legion quartered among the Nervii. The Nervii were an enterprising, and at one time huge, tribe of Belgians which in 57 BC had ambushed Caesar's legions and come within a hair's breadth of putting an end to Caesar's Gallic campaign and to Caesar himself. Frenetic bravery on the part of both Caesar and the legions had forestalled that disaster, but the Nervii, though defeated and bloody, were only temporarily bowed. All they needed was a new leader. This they got in full measure in the shape of Ambiorix, chief of the Eborones, who came to them leading a group of Gallic tribes with jaw-breaking names and exhibiting an impressive supply of fiery rhetoric. These speeches were not strictly accurate, as they alluded to Germans pouring across the Rhine and a general uprising of Gauls against the Romans, but Ambiorix, like any wily politician, never let truth stand in the way of his making a point. These little gems of rhetoric served to fire up the various tribes and to put Marcus Cicero in serious danger of being one brother short.

The collected tribes attacked Cicero's men who were out foraging for timber, and the Romans took what wood they had gathered and broke all speed records getting back to camp and setting up towers and fortifications with said timber. Cicero's forces found themselves in the unenviable position of having to fight all day and work on fortifications all night. Quintus might have been short both in stature and in temper and a great one for feeling picked on, but he was no weakling; although he was sick, he worked alongside the men. He was no fool either, and when the Nervii who were best acquainted with him asked for a truce and offered the Romans safe passage out of their territory, he was not deceived for an instant as to just how far out of their territory they meant to escort him. He said that Romans didn't negotiate with enemies under arms and promised to intercede with Caesar for them if they decided to be sensible.

Next the Gauls tried some of the tactics they had learned from the Romans; they set up a rampart and dug a fortification ditch. Since they had no spades and had to cut the sod with their swords, they no doubt found this borrowed tactic a bit of a chore, but they persevered. When a strong wind arose, however, they had the happy thought that throwing burning javelins into the straw roofs of the Roman huts inside the fort might be faster and more effective than siege works, besides being a heck of a lot less work. Soon they had an impressive little conflagration going in the Roman camp.

Ignoring the blaze behind them and the fact that whatever they had in the way of possessions was rapidly being reduced to cinders, the Romans fought boldly and beat back the enemy. Meanwhile they kept trying to send a message to Caesar, and the Gauls kept skewering their messengers, until a Nervian who was actually loyal to Quintus sent one of his slaves, who looked a lot like any other Gaul, ambling through the enemy lines with a message for Caesar attached to his javelin.

Caesar assembled an army with lightning speed and came to the rescue. The Gauls gave up blockading Quintus, as they didn't want to become the meat in a very uncomfortable sandwich, and charged out to meet Caesar. They suffered the fate common to so many armies that charged out to meet Caesar. Back in camp Marcus still had a brother, much the worse for wear, but alive.

There had been a sad lack of messages from Quintus, but this was not unusual, so back in good old Italy Marcus, who had never recovered from his disillusionment over the conference at Luca which had placed power firmly in the hands of the Triumvirate, busied himself with writing. He was now spending a good deal of his time in literary works such as a series of Scipionic dialogues: the now incomplete *De Republica* forms a part of this series. The *De Republica* has had a hard life: for centuries this search for the best form of government and examination of the bases of national prosperity was represented in world literature only by the *Somnium Scipionis*, which at an early date had been taken from the sixth book of this work and studied separately. Also belonging to this period of Cicero's life is the *De Legibus;* in this monologue he interspersed comments by Quintus and Atticus, and presented law as universally sanctioned by reason, which is a divine gift of Providence.

Worthy of special consideration by anyone interested in Cicero the man is *De Oratore.* This three-book work on oratory is written in the form of an imaginary discussion at the Tusculan villa of the great orator L. Crassus between Crassus, his rival M. Antonius, and a few others who had less to say. Antonius maintains that oratory can be studied apart from law, philosophy, and other disciplines, but Crassus expounds Cicero's own lofty view—that oratorical prowess should arise from deep knowledge, not shallow speaking tricks. Cicero's devotion to the highest principles, a devotion that often exposed him to danger and ultimately brought about his death, shines through.

Among Cicero's speeches during this period was the *Pro Milone,* a defense of the man who, to the relief of most honest and some not-so-honest citizens, had murdered Clodius Pulcher in January of 52 BC. (This couldn't have been too much of a shock to Rome, as thinking persons had always known that most likely somebody someday would murder Clodius.) Unfortunately, like Cicero's speech about the *Lex Campania*, his defense of Milo suffered from Triumvirate pruning. It was a subject to which he could really have warmed up, if Pompey's guards had not made it clear that Cicero had better not win this case. He wrote a very effective speech and afterwards sent it to Milo in Massilia, where he had retired in exile. Milo sent him a wry letter saying that he was glad Cicero had not delivered that speech in court, because if he had, as an acquitted man Milo would never have tasted the excellent seafood in Massilia.

About this time also Cicero freed (perhaps as a fiftieth birthday present), his lifelong slave, secretary, and literary advisor, Marcus Tullius Tiro. This outstanding man was not only intelligent and diligent, which is a rare enough combination, but was also totally devoted to the interests of the Cicero family. Since he was expected to record Cicero's many speeches, it is not surprising that he perfected a system of Latin shorthand, which he used to preserve all those magnificent but extremely numerous words of Cicero's fairly accurately. (A number of medieval manuscripts in "Tironian annotation" survive, containing many of the Cicero's speeches and indicating just how diligent poor, overworked Tiro was, as the list of extant speeches fills several volumes). Tiro, burning to do justice to Cicero's reputation, which took some nasty blows from time to time both before and after his death, also wrote a biography of Cicero and published Cicero's private letters, which one wonders if Cicero would have really wanted offered to the public, warts and all. Largely because of Tiro's untiring efforts, which cost him time and trouble and might have cost him his head as well in those uncertain days after Cicero's demise, we know more of Cicero than of any other Roman.

CHAPTER XII
GOING ABROAD

Iustitia, abstinentia, clementia tui Ciceronis opiniones omnium superavit.

The justice, restraint, and kindness of your Cicero surpassed the expectations of all.

Ad Atticum 16, 1–3

In 52 BC Cicero, delighted by his recent election to the position of augur,* was not nearly so delighted with a law fairly bursting with good intentions (which, like so many laws bursting with good intentions, produced some rather unsettling side effects). This law, duly brought forth and shepherded through the legislative process by those aforementioned Roman moralists, stipulated that a man who held the office of praetor or consul must wait five years before being assigned as governor of a province. The laudable objective of this legislation was to make it impractical for unscrupulous politicians to borrow the money to run for office with the plan of repaying the loan within two years by squeezing the hapless provincials in the lands they would be appointed to govern immediately after their year of office. This law had its desired effect, as borrowing money for five or six years was much more difficult than borrowing it for one. Unfortunately it also created a sudden shortage of ex-consuls and ex-praetors available to govern provinces, and for the next five years governors would have to be supplied from the backlog of ex-consuls and ex-praetors of five or more years standing. Cicero was a member *par excellence* of this group, and it was plain that he was bound for foreign duty. In July 51 BC, much to his disgust, he took up residence as governor of Cilicia in southern Asia Minor.

It is doubtful that his *joie de vivre* received much reinforcement from the family party he took along, which included not only his spoiled son Marcus Jr., but his brother Quintus as legate and Quintus Jr. The deplorable lack of harmony which plagued Cicero's family is evident in a letter to Atticus in which he described a little contretemps between Quintus and Pomponia at the villa in the old home town of Arpinum just before the party's departure (*Ad Atticum* 5.1). From Cicero's wistful comments in a letter to Terentia, we gather that Quintus, not content with arguing with his own wife, managed to squabble with Marcus' wife also. Terentia's personality, never exactly sparkling, had probably not been improved much by the attacks of "great pain of the joints" which Cicero had mentioned to Atticus some years earlier. Whether this phrase referred to arthritis, rheumatism, or gout, Terentia had personal discomfort and a hot-headed brother-in-law to contend with—not a pretty fate (*Ad Atticum* 1.5).

Young Quintus, who was constantly pulled back and forth in the full-scale civil war between his parents, by no stretch of the imagination could have been called a well-balanced child. Meanwhile Marcus Jr. was displaying the winning charm with which he often escaped the consequences of his willful nature. (A few years later he displayed this same winning charm when he renounced drinking and wild living, but unfortunately this renunciation had to be repeated rather often (*Ad Familiares* 16. 21). Cicero said of the pair of them that Marcus Jr. required the spur, and Quintus Jr. the curb, to make them run as good horses should. While Marcus Jr. seems to have taken to the spur well enough to preserve appearances during this Asian sojourn, Cicero found himself trying to apply the curb with less than spectacular results.

Cicero Proconsul, however, in spite of family distractions, carried out his responsibilities as governor carefully and with a scrupulous honesty that he boasted of in a letter to Atticus. Julius Caesar had enacted some pretty stringent (and pretty unpopular with the Senatorial set) restrictions on what governors could demand from provincials, but Cicero wrote that he had not even accepted the hay for his animals and other necessities that the Julian law allowed a governor to receive; he had paid for everything except four beds and a roof over his head, and sometimes even passed those things by and camped out. He proceeded, with his usual total lack of bashfulness, to say that provincials for miles around gathered just to wonder at his justice, abstinence, and kindness (*Ad Atticum* 5.16).

It was not surprising that Cicero came as a shock to the provincials, as the governor before him had been one of the Appii Claudii, and not one of the best of them (although not the worst: that honor was reserved for his despicable little brother, Clodius Pulcher). From Laodicea in February of 50 BC Cicero would write to Atticus that Appius, on the way home, had written to complain that Cicero had rescinded some of his decrees. Cicero said that Appius, having plundered the province to the point of exhausting it, could not bear to see Cicero relieve it, and Appius' friends were saying that Cicero was treating the province so well only to make Appius look bad (which, by all accounts, was not hard to do). Appius, to no one's surprise, was eventually prosecuted for the extortion carried out while he was governor. (One wonders how Roman courts had time to do anything besides prosecute larcenous governors.)

Immediately after his arrival in his province at the end of July, Cicero made a tour of the army encampments (always a wise move if a Roman governor wanted to be sure that the natives were not planning a few changes in the structure of the government and the status of the governor). He found the army placements satisfactory. Near the end of August, however, the always enterprising Parthians,* who had come into the region to give the city of Antioch a major headache, sent some troops over into Cicero's province of Cilicia on a little fishing expedition. The Roman troops in the area promptly cut them to ribbons, but Parthians on a fishing expedition were never good news, and Cicero, surveying the general situation, decided that for everybody's safety he had better reduce a mountainous region called Amanus from an enemy stronghold to a wildlife habitat. Showing the clever sneakiness that might have been expected of a leading practitioner of the law, he marched a day's journey away from his target and, just as the natives relaxed and went back to doing whatever they did when not attacking or being attacked, he brought his forces back under cover of night. Dawn on the morning of October 13 found Cicero and his troops halfway up the mountain and its defenders in big trouble. The Romans attacked in three sections, one commanded by Marcus and Quintus Cicero, and two others commanded by other legates of Cicero. Having eliminated most of the defenders of this stronghold, Cicero marched on a town with the interesting name of Pindenissus, which belonged to a tribe with the even more challenging name of Eleutherocilices. This was not by Roman standards exactly a metropolis, but what it lacked in size and grandeur it more than made up for in determination. Cicero laid siege to it with earthworks, towers, catapults and bowmen (all of which, he proudly boasted, cost his allies nothing) for 57 days before finally taking it. After receiving hostages from neighboring tribes, who had decided they did not want to court a similar visit from the Romans, he left his brother Quintus in charge of the army and returned to the capital to tend to state business.

In January of 50 BC, Cicero related the story of this momentous engagement in a letter to Cato, whom he was importuning to speak in the Senate in favor of granting Cicero a *supplicatio*,* or official thanksgiving, for the victory. (This may seem strange to some who recall that Cicero had poked fun at Cato in some of his speeches. Cicero did not expect any animosity from this, and it appears that Cato did not harbor any. Perhaps, as the forerunners of modern politicians, the movers and shakers of Rome knew how little politicians' words really mean.) Cato replied dryly that he had done so, although to declare a *supplicatio* would be to thank the gods for a service to Rome which Cicero himself had provided by his prudence and self-control. He also warned Cicero that a *supplicatio* was by no means a forerunner to a triumph,* which Cato very clearly saw that Cicero desired with all his glory-loving heart. He grumbled a bit about the fact that, in his humble opinion, it was a much greater honor for the Senate to declare that a province had been safe-guarded by the uprightness and mildness of its governor than by the favor of heaven or the strength of an army. Nevertheless, he wished Cicero well, asked for his continued esteem, and exhorted him to continue on the way home to use his energy and integrity to win more allies to Rome. (Roman officials suffered from no lack of energy, but integrity to go with it was harder to come by.)

From Cilicia Cicero somehow found time to write to his young protégée Caelius (the same whom he had defended in the *Pro Caelio*). We may recall Cicero's less than enthusiastic attitude about beast shows which had surfaced in the Marius letter about the opening of Pompey's theater; in one of the Caelius letters there is plain evidence that his attitude had not changed. Caelius, who was serving as curule aedile, had requested that Cicero ship him some panthers from Cilicia for use in the gladiatorial arena. Cicero said that the panthers had complained that they were the only beings who were being plotted against during Cicero's governorship, and moved over into Caria; therefore he was unable to accommodate Caelius (*Ad Familiares* 2.11).

Though he wrote insistent letters to everyone whom he believed might possibly have influence in seeing that his term of office was not extended, Cicero discharged his duties with meticulous and even enthusiastic consideration for the welfare of the province. He not only curtailed his own expenses, but firmly refused any of the expensive honors which provincials often felt bound to offer to their Roman governors, such as statues, shrines, and sculptured chariots. He insisted that they honor him only with speeches (rightly reflecting that fine talk is not expensive). He also persuaded wealthy Romans and Greeks living in the area to relieve the suffering provincials during a famine, and achieved this outstanding feat without expenditure of anything but a great deal of his personal influence (and, according to *Ad Atticum* 5.21, perhaps a few promises for political favors back in the old metropolis. In addition he managed to remove or at least reduce the load of debt that the various regions bore by two measures: first, his governorship caused them no expense at all, and second, he managed to corral the corruption of the local native magistrates (*Ad Atticum* 6.2).

Much to his relief, (and partially through the influence of Atticus, which he had enlisted as soon as he found out he was bound for foreign parts), Cicero's year of governorship was not extended. At the same time he was pleasantly surprised by the realization that Quintus Jr., who could be counted on to do the unexpected, had contrived to reconcile his warring parents (*Ad Atticum* 6.7).

After some time in Greece, where he was forced to leave his beloved secretary Tiro on account of illness, Cicero returned to Rome only to discover that matters at home had not exactly prospered in his absence. While enroute home, on the island of Rhodes he received the news that Terentia, over his objection, had approved a marriage between Tullia (who was now free again) and a young Roman noble named Dolabella whose chief claims to fame were his dissipation and his chronic state of debt (*Ad Atticum* 6.6). This marriage was less than happy, and Cicero complained bitterly that this was just one of the family affairs Terentia had mismanaged while he had been away. His temper was not improved by the discovery that hopes for a triumphal parade were eluding him, although through the efforts of various people, including Cato, the Senate had declared a *supplicatio* for his rather minor victory, and he could now as a victorious general claim the title of *imperator*.* He kept the withered victory laurels on his attendants' staffs in vain. But his personal grievances paled before the appalling discovery that he had arrived just in time for the grand opening of the civil war between Caesar and Pompey.

The First Triumvirate had struggled along for some years (in spite of the best efforts of Clodius Pulcher to make all three members suspicious of each other), but one of its strongest props had always been the marriage of Caesar's only child Julia to Pompey. Her death in 54 BC had left them with no real tie, and Crassus had not helped matters in 53 BC by going off to war against the Parthians and getting himself killed, as did so many noble Romans who went off to war against the Parthians. No three-legged stool fares well when one of its legs turns up missing, and it is not surprising that the First Triumvirate took a tumble. Thus Cicero arrived in the Old Home Town to discover that he was going to have to make a choice, and it wasn't likely to be a pretty one.

By the year 50 BC, the Senate and the jealous Pompey had become enraged and fearful as Caesar sent more and more rich prizes of war to Rome. After nine years in Gaul, he had added an area to the Roman holdings that was roughly one-third the size of the whole empire, and it was an area largely loyal to Caesar personally. As the years passed, the Senate and Pompey were less and less thrilled with Caesar's reports from the front, especially those such as the one concerning Bratuspantium.* The leaders of this enterprising little city, when they heard that Caesar was coming, having taken a thoughtful look at his record thus far, simply sent envoys to him and surrendered to him before he got there. He had proved to be both a formidable enemy and a generous overlord, so they felt they might just as well skip the formalities and get down to the foreign aid package.

Matters there and elsewhere in Gaul had been settled very satisfactorily, at least in the opinion of everyone except the Senate. A conquering general was bad enough, but a conquering general at whom both the conquered peoples and the general public threw roses and compliments was unendurable. They had never encountered anyone who seemed more likely to turn into a *rex*.

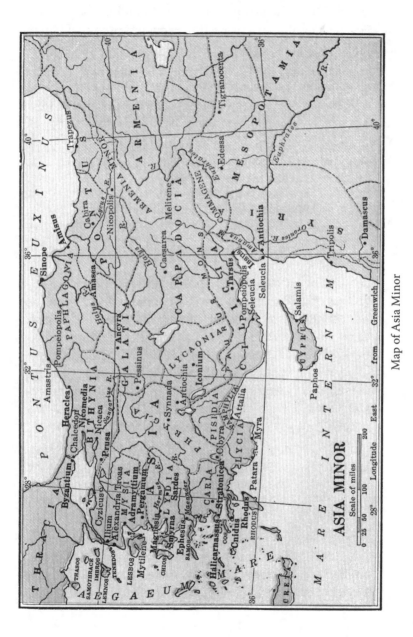

Map of Asia Minor

CHAPTER XIII
EVERYTHING COMES UNGLUED

Silent leges inter arma.
The laws are silent in times of war.
Pro Milone, 11

O n January 1, 49 BC the senate ordered Caesar to disband his legions at the little Rubicon River, which marked the boundary between Cisalpine Gaul and Italy, and come into Rome alone. Caesar knew that the Senate in order to be rid of him would employ any means, some of which might be decidedly injurious to his health and well-being. Having resolved not to present an easy target by setting out for Rome alone, he crossed the Rubicon at the head of his army. This was quite enough to start a war. Pompey was put in charge of the Senatorial forces, such as they were, and the struggle was on. Marcus' brother Quintus, although he had served as legate under Caesar in Gaul from 54–51 BC and had won great praise for his achievements, went with his son to join the forces of Pompey. As Caesar advanced south toward Rome, Pompey and his senatorial army, along with many senators who supported him, discovered that they had sudden business down in Brundisium. Marcus Cicero, left in the Campania south of Rome by these fast-moving senators, was charged with protecting the city of Capua and its surrounding district for the Senatorial cause, yet he was in correspondence with both sides. It seems that while all these stirring events were taking shape, both Cicero and Cato, who were intelligent enough to recognize looming disaster when they saw it, tried hard to stay out of a situation that promised destruction on all sides without any good results. As so often happens in such a fracas, however, thanks to their friends, their good sense never had a chance. Both were eventually sucked into the vortex of Civil War.

Cicero looked to that son-in-law he had not wanted, Dolabella, who was high in Caesar's good graces, to safeguard Tullia and Terentia in Rome. This proved to be very little strain on Dolabella. Even if Caesar was no great mathematician, he had enough arithmetic to know that every time either side in a civil war killed a man, Rome was a soldier short. Thus he was extremely reluctant to engage in civil war, being well versed in the horror stories from the time of Marius and Sulla. Again and again he offered peace overtures to Pompey (who evidently didn't have the same view of those horror stories) without success. Much to Cicero's dismay Pompey fled ever southward as Caesar determinedly advanced. Caesar's generosity in success, as he moved down the peninsula of Italy, wrung this cry from Cicero: "By Hercules if he will kill no one, if he will take nothing from anybody, those who greatly feared him will greatly love him" (*Ad Atticum* 8. 13). Looking over the Senatorial forces under Pompey, who were cruel and arrogant to the people and very ill-prepared for war, he would soon say "Nothing was good except the cause" (*Ad Familiares* 7.3). Yet he could not desert his cherished dream of the Old Republic. He told Atticus that he passed the time, which hung heavy on his hands and other body parts, debating with himself in both Greek and Latin on questions of political ethics. Slaves going dutifully about their business and suddenly discovering the orator striding back and forth arguing both sides of ethical questions in two languages must have received a severe shock.

As Cicero carried on his bilingual debates and tried to keep his spirits up, his nephew Quintus Jr. was keeping the family news lively. Cicero answered what was evidently a plea from Uncle Atticus to use his influence with the boy by stating that he was doing his best, but that every time he tried to "tighten the rein" on the youngster, as Atticus was evidently doing when he had Quintus Jr. in charge, Quintus Sr. stepped in. From various other comments it is obvious that the boy was as devious as a politician and handled his parents like a circus ringmaster (*Ad Atticum* 10.6). Also, he was secretive and appeared to be full of mysterious plans (*Ad Atticum* 10.10). In contrast to Marcus Jr., who was easily corrected by his father, Young Quintus was surly, haughty and aggressive. Cicero still hoped that discipline might correct his faults, if only Quintus Sr. would stop indulging him and allow some of that discipline. He said that Quintus Sr. himself was often angry with his relations, but loved them all deeply and could easily be turned back to them with one conversation (*Ad Atticum* 10.11). It seems that Young Quintus was a tiger of a different stripe.

Pompey fled to Greece. Caesar did not follow immediately; he went first to Spain to deal with senatorial forces there. He made various requests to Cicero to help him or at least to remain neutral. These requests were vigorously reinforced by the pleas of young Caelius, who was with Caesar (*Ad Familiares* 8.16).

Caesar proceeded around the Empire defeating and pardoning the senatorial troops. Commenting on the fact that these pardoned fellows usually galloped right off to join another senatorial troop, Caesar said in a letter to Cicero "They must be what they are; I must be what I am" (*Ad Atticum* 9. 16). A number of Romans, including Cicero, would have been much happier if they had known exactly what that was.

Cicero finally crossed the Adriatic to join Pompey in Greece. Carefully looking over the troops and comparing them with Roman armies he had known, Cicero decided that victory over Caesar was a pipedream for the motley Pompeian forces. With their arrogance, their cruelty, and their desire to fight chiefly inspired by a hope of freeing themselves of their huge debts, they reminded him forcibly of Catiline's followers. Fatigue and worry, and perhaps a close-up view of his Republican cohorts, made him ill, and he withdrew from the battle plans. Defeated at Pharsalus, Pompey fled to Egypt, where the youthful pharaoh, Ptolemy Auletes, killed him.

While Caesar mopped up the remaining pockets of resistance, Cicero, who, being ill, had missed the battle of the Titans at Pharsalus, cooled his heels in Brundisium for eleven months, wondering if he had finally put himself in Caesar's black books forever. (His daughter Tullia came and stayed with him; this both gave him comfort and increased his guilty feeling that he had brought great trouble on her.

A short and formal letter to Terentia in Rome made it clear that his wife's company he could well do without.)

Not only had Cicero finally backed the wrong horse, but his brother Quintus had become enraged with him for some reason he never fully explained. Both Quintus Sr. and Jr. abused Cicero to Caesar and could have endangered his very life. Caesar, who was not without experience in the realm of unreasonable attacks, exercised his well-known clemency and simply overlooked the whole affair (*Ad Atticum* 11. 8).

In September of 47 BC Caesar at last came to Brundisium. In those days Caesar seldom had any trouble making a fair guess at what other people were thinking, and he knew Cicero very well. When he saw Cicero coming to meet him, probably with something of the manner of a prize hunting dog which knows it hasn't lived up to its potential and expects to be sent to the nearest animal shelter, he went down to meet the orator and walked a good distance with him talking privately. The conqueror showed every sign of respect and friendship for the orator. Perhaps Cicero entertained a few rueful thoughts about how different his reception might have been if he had joined the Caesarian forces and had had to face a victorious Pompey.

CHAPTER XIV
CAESAR SUPREME

*Homines enim ad deos nulla re propius accedunt quam
salutem hominibus dando.*

For men are never so like the gods as when
they rescue their fellow men.

Pro Ligario, 38

When, after more fighting in Africa, Caesar finally returned to Italy in 46 BC, he took time from a rather hectic
schedule to see Cicero and effect a formal reconciliation.
This left Cicero free to enter Rome. Once there Cicero wrote to Aulus
Caecina, anxiously waiting in exile to see if Caesar would pardon him,
that Caesar, who had a nature naturally placable and kindly, had been
faithfully adhering to his well-known policy of clemency. He expressed
astonishment at Caesar's fairness and wisdom, at his pardoning Quintus Cicero and dozens of other Pompeian adherents who survived the
war, and at his making many of the former Pompeians, such as Brutus
and Cassius, governors.

Cicero knew, however, that his independent political wings had
definitely been clipped. He broke a long public silence in September
of 46 BC when in a speech he expressed his fervent admiration for
Caesar's generous pardoning of Marcus Claudius Marcellus, an arrogant and insufferable opponent Caesar might have been forgiven
for stifling.

Also in 46 BC, Cicero divorced Terentia for "inattention to his
interests" after thirty years of a married life that had always been
somewhat acerbic. Soon after his divorce he married his young ward
Publilia, which proved to be a mistake. When the death of his beloved

daughter Tullia in 45 BC left him inconsolable, Publilia was no help whatever, and another divorce was in the making.

Cicero wrote to his friend Servius Sulpicius that he was now bereft of both republic and daughter, in a time when either could have offered him consolation for the loss of the other. He said that he must now learn how to live a quiet life under the absolute domination of a man who was wise, liberal, and very fond of him, but who maintained a complete control over everything that was galling to the republican Roman spirit.

CHAPTER XV
THE DENOUEMENT

Defendi rem publicam adulescens; non deseram senex
I defended the republic as a young man; I shall not desert her
now that I am old.

Philippicae II, 118

When everything and everybody has failed a literary man, he has one last resource. As time passed, the grieving and disillusioned Cicero was able to return to his writing, and found respite in a flurry of literary activity. Among his many writings of this time are the *Brutus*, or *De Claris Oratoribus*, a history of Roman oratory in dialogue form, and the *Orator ad M. Brutum*, which seeks to delineate the perfect orator. (Cicero is credited by many scholars with enriching the Latin language and making it a marvelous vehicle for communication for the ages. This ability of his makes it very hard for us to excuse him for writing three major works with almost the same name. Perhaps students will be saved from terminal high blood pressure if they remember that the earlier work *De Oratore* is a discussion of what is involved in oratory, while the *Brutus*, or *De Claris Oratoribus*, is a record of actual achievement, and the *Orator ad M. Brutum* is a hypothetical discussion of the ideal orator.)

We observe with relief that the literary effort to which we next turn our attention has a title totally free from any form of the word "orator." The *Tusculanae Disputationes* discuss how man may best deal with death, pain, grief, passion and other matters exceedingly likely to make him uncomfortable, but at least they don't tell him how to make a speech.

In the period immediately before and after the assassination of
Julius Caesar, Cicero withdrew from Rome and immersed himself in
writing letters of advice to friends and colleagues and in producing
more literature. Outstanding among his products in this period is
the *Laelius* or *De Amicitia,* one of the world's finest and best written essays on friendship. For this literary exercise Cicero certainly
had plenty of raw material. All he had to do was take a good look at
Atticus, to whom the work was dedicated, and then take a look at the
other important people in his life, all of whom had failed him in one
way or another.

Like some of Cicero's earlier other philosophical treatises, this
one is written as a dialogue, a form dear to the hearts of the Greeks,
who believed that it most nearly represented thought processes
stimulated by interaction, real or imaginary. Cicero, ever a mixture
of statesman and dramatist, also liked its opportunities for adding
dramatic interest and for smoothly interpolating persons and events
from life. The main spokesman in the *De Amicitia* is Laelius, who is
represented as having a private discussion with his two sons-in-law,
Caius Fannius and Quintus Mucius Scaevola, soon after the death
of Scipio Africanus Minor, whose friendship with Laelius had been
famous. True to Cicero's high principles, Laelius insists that friendship exists between two people largely because of their natures, and
is only possible between the good, i.e. those who possess integrity,
fairness and kindness and are free from greed, lust and rash temper. (This last reflection was probably suggested by the personality of
his brother Quintus, whose temper caused all his relationships to go
away sooner or later.) If this sounds more like a recipe for sainthood
than a formula for friendship, we must remember that the absence
of any of the positive qualities listed, or the presence of any of the
negative ones, is likely to poke a hole in friendship's little boat before
it gets out of the harbor.

It is fitting that the *De Officiis* was the last of Cicero's philosophical works. It not only further polished Cicero's creation of a philosophical vocabulary for Latin (which it had sadly lacked heretofore)
but also set out the moral views of a practical but high-minded politician. He dedicated this work to his son, hoping to imbue the young

man with his own belief that no personal or material advantage is worth the sacrifice of one's integrity. In spite of the great price he had paid, and the greater one he was soon to pay, for his determination to do what he thought was right, he still believed that in the last analysis honor and expediency will be one and the same, for the dishonorable course will not in the long run be expedient.

The assassination of Julius Caesar on March 15, 44 BC, cast Cicero into transports of joy which made his recent panegyrics on Caesar sound hypocritical, but this was not necessarily the case. It was not difficult for a man like Cicero to hold several contradictory opinions at the same time. He sincerely admired Caesar's mildness and generosity in victory, and was perfectly capable of having convinced himself that Caesar, once the political situation and he himself were secure, might lay down his power as Sulla had. Those rose-colored glasses of Cicero's, which had given him such a strikingly errant picture of the Grand Old Senate, could certainly have done the same for Caesar. Cicero never saw, as Caesar so clearly did, that the Senate of 45 BC was manifestly unfit to rule the *orbis terrarum.** What Caesar did for Rome, and the further things he proposed to do, Cicero was constitutionally incapable of fully appreciating because they could not take place within the old power structure. When Caesar was murdered, Cicero had had plenty of time to see that Caesar had no intention of laying down power, and thus he rejoiced in the assassination.

It soon became clear that this assassination, however, left the Optimates, among whom Cicero was once again a leader, with some thorny problems. They hated to condemn the conspirators, who were their colleagues and who had their sneaking sympathy, as murderers. If they hailed them as deliverers, however, they had a raging mob of Romans just outside the Curia to deal with. To make matters worse, the sole remaining consul after Caesar's unexpected demise was Mark Antony, who had long been high in Caesar's command, and had an eye to power for himself. He hastened to remind them that such a hailing would render Caesar accursed and all his acts by which everyone had benefited null and void. Some of those whom Caesar had helped would not even be senators any more; many would lose their offices. Furthermore, the crowd of Caesar's veterans gathering in the city day by day would be more than likely to create a catastrophe that everyone preferred not to contemplate.

In this crisis Cicero proved that he had not wasted his time in Greece. He recalled that in Old Athens a "forgetting" had sometimes been proclaimed; this meant that both sides agreed to forget the recent past and take no vengeance for it. (Political enemies still use this procedure after they have exhausted all possible means of doing each other in; it doesn't mean much today, and it didn't mean much then, but it is a great way of getting past the moment.) That satisfied the senate, which was soon to learn that the ordinary Roman had little patience with such political refinements. The people's anger was red-hot, and the public funeral oration that the senate allowed Antony to give for Caesar stoked this fire that needed no stoking. Antony reminded the people of all Caesar's mighty deeds and capped this moving speech by reading Caesar's will, in which he had left for each Roman from his fortune a monetary gift equaling several weeks' wages. That did it. The conspirators fled to the provinces for cover.

A thoughtful look at Mark Antony, who was now in a position of great power, was enough to make Romans have second thoughts about the wisdom of ridding themselves of Caesar. An ambitious man totally lacking in Caesar's kindlier qualities, Antony was an able soldier and a skilled speaker who might well command the loyalty of Caesar's followers. He was also a prime example of the nastier breed of military types, firmly believing that in that fine old proverb, "the only good enemy is a dead enemy." If he consolidated his hold, there would be none of that nonsense about clemency for those who had opposed him. Realizing that Antony held four aces, Cicero denounced him in a fiery set of speeches known as the Philippics, so named because the Greek Demosthenes had favored Phillip II of Macedon with a similar set of uncomplimentary remarks. These succeeded so well in pointing out that Antony fell lamentably short of being a replacement for Julius Caesar that Antony fled, muttering curses against Cicero.

When Caesar's heir Octavian came to Rome, Cicero was happy to join the Senate's advances to the boy, saying that Octavian had written and asked that Cicero join him and save the state a second time. Ecstatic that the young man knew about the Catilinarian conspiracy,

Cicero immediately developed a high opinion of his discernment. The Senate named Octavian pro-praetor. He soon set forth with the consuls-elect Hirtius and Pansa to do battle with Antony, who with his army was near Modena in northern Italy. Antony retreated into Gaul, regrouped, and returned to find Octavian, now consul, waiting for him with an even larger army than he had sent earlier. Just as Cicero and the Senate had settled back to watch Octavian destroy Antony, they learned that Lepidus had brokered another Triumvirate composed of Antony, Octavian, and his peerless self. It suddenly became clear to an appalled government that Octavian had used the backing of the senate to help him force Antony to join him in destroying the murderers of his adoptive father, which was the first item on his extensive agenda.

Octavian and Antony were soon hot on the trail of Brutus, Cassius, and the rest of the conspirators who had brought Julius Caesar's adventures to such an abrupt and messy conclusion. When the battle of Philippi had taken care of the major conspirators, the Triumvirate published a proscription list of Romans who were to be murdered and whose property would be confiscated. Among the doomed were both Marcus and Quintus Cicero. Octavian evidently was not especially enamored of Quintus, but he fought to save Marcus Cicero. Unfortunately Mark Antony was determined, quite literally, to have his head, and his name remained on the list.

Quintus Cicero and his son, who had done little to endear themselves to their relatives, much less their dependents, were unceremoniously betrayed by their slaves and killed. When Marcus Cicero heard about the proscription at his villa at Tusculum, with the aid of his faithful slaves, he made an attempt to escape by sea, but gave it up and came back. The next day his slaves persuaded him to leave again and carried him in a litter through his lovely gardens. The assassins, sent by Antony and led by a centurion named Herennius, overtook him. Cicero saw them coming and commanded the slaves to set down the litter. He looked his murderer steadfastly in the eye, then stretched out his neck. Those nearby covered their faces as Herennius slew him and, in accord with Antony's orders, cut off his head and the hands by which the Philippics were written. Once again Cicero's impassioned words befitted his fate: "Indeed I might even wish for death, after all that I have accomplished and all that I have borne. Two things only I long for: one, that in dying I might leave the Roman people free (for the immortal gods could give me no greater gift), and two, that each man may receive exactly what he deserves for the way he has treated his country." (*Second Philippic Oration on Mark Antony*) It might seem that in the short run this dying prayer had not been answered. Antony joined Octavian in a widespread war that felled the remnants of the Republican army and broke the power of the Roman Senate forever. But Antony consistently underrated Octavian, who soon dispensed with Antony and his possible successors in no uncertain manner and became for all practical purposes Emperor of Rome. He then chose Cicero's son (who had had the good fortune to be in Greece when the most prominent members of his family had lost their heads) as co-consul with him and allotted to him the tasks of announcing to the Senate Antony's defeat and of destroying Antony's statues. Even Cicero might have felt that Antony had received what he deserved, and the Roman people, though perhaps not free in the way Cicero had meant, entered into the long glorious period known as the *Pax Romana*.*

Years later Octavian, now Augustus, found his grandson reading Cicero's works in the garden. The boy, well aware of the horrendous story of the proscriptions and attacked by an understandable trepidation, tried to conceal the book under his tunic. Augustus, taking it from him, turned through a large part of it thoughtfully, and at last returned it with a statement that might well serve as Cicero's epitaph: "An eloquent man, my boy, and a lover of his country." (Plutarch's *Lives*, "Cicero")

APPENDIX I
DEFINITIONS AND EXPLANATIONS

Academic: a follower of the teachings of Plato, who had taught the sciences and philosophy; so named from their place of meeting, the Academy.

aedile: a magistrate charged with the care of public buildings, markets, grain supply, games, and theatrical productions.

Assembly of the Roman People: The Roman Assembly, or *comitia centuriata,* elected magistrates, passed or rejected measures proposed to it by officials or the Senate, tried capital crimes, and decided war or peace. It was convened by a consul or a tribune and could only vote on matters presented to it. Caesar presented measures to it which traditionally should have been offered by the Senate.

augur: One of the college of priests who divined the will of the gods by observing signs or omens, especially in the behavior of fowls both domestic and wild. Whether the chickens ate, and how they ate, indicated whether any action, military or otherwise, could be undertaken with hope of success. One frustrated Roman general, when informed that the sacred chickens would not eat, shouted, "Then let them drink," and threw them overboard. He lost his battle, and all the augurs looked incredibly smug.

Bratuspantium: City in Gaul belonging to the Bellovaci. When Caesar approached it with his army, it sent envoys out to him to surrender. (*De Bello Gallico* II, 13)

Catones and Scipiones: The Catones, not only the one we met pouring forth rhetoric in the Senate, but his ancestor Cato the Censor, lived appallingly honest and simple lives. As a military commander, Cato the Censor had been tough, fair, and thrifty; as a governor, he had traveled on foot with one slave; as a farmer, he had worked beside his slaves and had eaten whatever they ate. Scipio Africanus had gone to Spain as commander and had impressed the Spaniards equally with his skill at war and his chivalry when confronted with helpless captives. He had crowned all this by ignoring all the great opportunities for enriching himself and sleeping on a pallet of straw.

censor: One of two Roman magistrates elected every five years to take the census and to censor morals. Their term of office was eighteen months, which was time enough to count the people and make plenty of unpopular pronouncements about the failings of the populace. Their name and their functions give us two rather scary modern words—censor and census.

Cicero's Poetry: *"O fortunatam natam me consule Romam!"* The English translation is "O Rome, fortunate to be born in my consulship!" It refers to Cicero's quelling of the Catilinarian conspiracy, by which he believed that he had saved the Roman Republic from destruction. Still, to claim that a city that had been around for at least 650 years before his birth was born in his consulship was a bit much.

client: a Roman citizen who entrusted himself to another (usually a patrician) and received protection in return. The client helped his patron in political and private life and showed him respect, in return for which he received daily food or money when necessary and assistance in the courts.

constitution: Historians often refer to some political move in Rome as "unconstitutional." While this is a convenient way to say that someone was acting against the laws of Rome, it is not strictly accurate. The Romans did not, as the United States does, have a written constitution. They had the Law of the Twelve Tables as well as a large body of laws passed by their Senate and Assembly and a long list of previous judicial decisions. This is what is meant by the "Roman constitution."

consul: one of the two highest magistrates of the Roman Republic, elected annually to serve for one year. The two consuls were equal in power and commanded the army on alternate days. In case of two enemies attacking at once (which was not unlikely in the Roman Republic's turbulent life), each commanded an army. This novel system virtually guaranteed that Roman wars, even if unsuccessful, were unlikely to be boring.

cursus honorum: the order of offices sought and held as elective Roman magistracies. In the basic pattern, after military service, a man served as quaestor, praetor, consul, and then censor.

dictator: In old Republican Rome this official was appointed by the Senate to hold absolute power for six months to deal with some crisis, after which he laid down his power. Cincinnatus established the record for brevity, as he flattened Rome's enemies in sixteen days and then gave up the office in order to get back to his farm duties. As the old system sprang a few leaks, however, dictators did not always abide by the rules.

Disraeli and Gladstone: Benjamin Disraeli, a Conservative, and William Gladstone, a Whig or Liberal, both served as party leaders and as Prime Minister of England during a turbulent period of British politics from 1868–1880. Lord Granville, one of their contemporaries wrote: "Lord Beaconsfield [Disraeli] and Mr. Gladston are men of extraordinary ability; they dislike each other more than is usual among public men. Disraeli has the power of saying in two words that which drives a person of Mr. Gladstone's peculiar temperament into a state of great excitement." (Source: BBC Homepage History)

Fury: one of the female demon-deities who had snakes for hair and eyes that wept tears of blood. They were sent to punish the guilty, but sometimes also did in the innocent. The Dread Trio of these was made up of Tisiphone, Allecto, and Megaera. At times the more pessimistic of the Greeks and Romans spoke of a great many of these (people who encountered them were too distraught to take an accurate head count). They could change shape and appearance, with each form raging about and frothing at the mouth worse than the previous ones.

imperator: title of honor given a victorious Roman general either by acclamation by his troops or by a senatorial decree. Later it became identified with the emperor.

legate: a senatorial member of a provincial governor's staff who in Cicero's time was often used as commander of individual legions or detachments.

Mithradates VI: king of Pontus. Legend remembers him for his cunning and courage in his long battle against the Romans, and for his unusual mode of self-protection. He had for years taken small doses of every known poison until he was immune to them all and could eat and drink whatever was offered him. When defeat at Pompey's hands gave him a wish to die, he found this immunity inconvenient—he was forced to employ a slave with a sharp sword to send him to his questionable eternal reward.

Mucius Scaevola: This legendary Roman hero took exception to the fact that Lars Porsenna, king of the Etruscans and cousin of Tarquin the Arrogant, came down in 509 BC with an army larger than the entire population of the new Roman Republic to force the Romans to take back his appalling cousin as King of Rome. Mucius sneaked into the Etruscan camp and killed the most elaborately dressed man he saw, who turned out to be the king's secretary. While explaining this little *faux pas* to the irate king, he was threatened with torture. In response to this attempt to browbeat him, he thrust his right hand into a handy burning brazier and held it there, recommending that King Porsenna take note of the Roman attitude toward pain. The message was not lost on Porsenna. He decided that Tarquin, whom he had probably had difficulty liking anyway, could fend for himself. Sending

Mucius, who had now earned the nickname of Lefty, home, Porsenna lifted the siege of Rome.

novus homo: new man; first of his family to hold a Roman curule office.

orbis terrarum: literally, "the circle of the lands" (usually around the Mediterranean Sea). For the Romans, the world.

Parthians: a confederacy of semi-nomadic tribes living in Asia Minor. They were excellent horsemen, famed for shooting arrows back over their shoulders as they rode away at full speed. This habit, while definitely showy, must have contributed to the need for chiropractors in their society.

patron: a Roman, usually a patrician, who assumed the protection of other citizens.

Pax Romana: During his long reign, Augustus established the *Pax Augusta,* which would expand into the two-hundred-year *Pax Romana,* or Roman peace, arguably the longest period of peace ever enjoyed by so large a section of the world. The *Pax Romana* was by no means a total absence of war but, according to some rhapsodic poets near its end, a period when a great overseeing government generally sought the welfare of the general populace, allowing many peoples to go about life's business safely under its wide umbrella.

praetor: in Cicero's time, one of the eight judges elected annually to serve for one year. They normally governed a province in the year following their praetorship.

Pompey's theater: Pompey built the first permanent theater in Rome in 55 BC. Before that time temporary theaters had been built for games and spectacles. There was much criticism of Pompey's frivolous building project, which was considered a scandalous waste of good marble. To still the complaining tongues, Pompey built a small temple to

Venus into his edifice and declared it sacred. He then consecrated it with the plays, games and beast hunts which Cicero pronounces less than successful.

quaestors: financial officers elected by the Roman Assembly and assigned to Rome or one of the various provinces or areas; this was the first elective office in the *cursus honorum.*

res publica: This phrase, which literally means "the public matter," was used by the Romans to mean the state, the country, or the government.

Romulus: the legendary founder of Rome and her first king.

rostra: the speaker's platform in front of the Roman Senate house. It was so called because it was decorated with prows *(rostra)* of ships. Since these prows were usually bronze beaks specially fashioned to ram a hole into the side of an enemy ship, they probably prevented the Masses from crowding too close to the speakers.

salutatio: formal morning reception at the house of important Romans; typically when clients greeted their patrons, made requests and received handouts. They might also find themselves recipients of a little assignment.

Senate: Originating as the council of the Roman kings, the senators (old men) became the principal governing body of the Roman state. The *patres,* or aristocratic senators, claimed descent from the oldest families. Men elected to major office became *patres conscripti* (enrolled).

Senate house: Generally, Senate meetings were held in the Curia, or Senate house, in the valley of the Forum. On November 8, 63 BC, the Roman Senate did not meet in the Curia. It met instead in the Temple of Jupiter Stator, which had, like most pagan temples, a high entrance with many steps and a narrow central hall. This seemed a safer place than the Senate House in view of the circumstances. Besides, it had the dubious guardianship of the Head God.

Stoic: a follower of the teachings of Zeno, so named from the *Stoa,* or porch, where Zeno taught. He taught that men should be free from joy or grief and consider virtue the highest good; this philosophy was very attractive to the Romans, and had many followers. Some of them followed from quite a distance, however, finding that constant virtue could be a bit trying.

supplicatio: a special time of adoration of the gods which could be decreed either in time of great peril or great triumph. Some of Caesar's victories were awarded *supplicationes* of fifteen days or more.

toga virilis: the plain white toga, badge of the Roman citizen, which a young man received at his coming-of-age ceremony. Immature boys and elected politicians wore a purple stripe on the toga; this system of classification gives us new respect for the intuitive wisdom of Romans.

triumph: a formal procession of a victorious Roman general along the Via Sacra to the temple of Jupiter Capitolinus. The triumph was granted by senatorial decree to a successful general in a *bellum iustum* (legitimate war). The official conditions for granting a triumph were: 1) the general undertook the war under favorable auspices (no drowning of the sacred chickens if he didn't like the omens); 2) the war was against a foreign enemy; 3) at least 5,000 of the enemy were slain, with relatively few Roman casualties; 4) he had been a dictator, consul, or praetor. As Roman history rolled along, some of these provisions got scant observance.

Vigintiviri: This phrase, literally meaning "twenty men," refers in this instance to the commission appointed to carry out Caesar's Campanian land distribution in 59 BC. Such naming was common among the Romans, cf. Decemviri, the ten men who wrote the Law of the Twelve Tables, the two very well-known sets of Triumviri, and the Duumviri, two-man committees appointed from time to time to carry out various projects of the Roman government.

APPENDIX II
MAJOR WORKS AND EVENTS
IN CICERO'S LIFE

MAJOR EVENTS

106 BC Marcus Tullius Cicero born at Arpinum, January 3.

102 BC Quintus Cicero born. Marius defeats the Teutones.

101 BC Marius defeats the Cimbri.

100 BC Julius Caesar born.

91 BC Cicero comes of age; that is, he assumes the *toga virilis*.*

90 BC The Social War. Citizenship granted to Italian allies at the close of the war.

89 BC Cicero serves in the army—for the first and last time.

88 BC Civil War. Sulla is victorious over Marius.

87 BC Marius returns to Rome.

MAJOR WORKS

(This list includes only writings that are extant in the whole or a large part. Works are placed across from the date of production with the exception of the eight-hundred sixty-four letters that span a quarter century from 68–43 BC and that are described below. Works without a synopsis are speeches.)

Epistulae ad Familiares: a collection arranged according to the persons to whom they are addressed. 16 books

Epistulae ad Atticum: Confidential letters to Cicero's friend Atticus. 16 books

Epistulae ad Quintum Fratrem: the entire published collection of letters written by Cicero to his brother. 3 books

Epistulae ad M. Brutum: an incomplete collection of letters written to Marcus Brutus. 2 books

De Inventione: a youthful treatise on rhetoric. c.90 BC

86 BC Marius dies.

83 BC Sulla returns to Italy. He posts his
proscription list.

82 BC Sulla becomes dictator.

81 BC Cicero defends Quinctius—his   *Pro Quinctio*
first case.

80 BC Cicero wins recognition by his   *Pro Roscio Amerino*
successful defense of Roscius.

79 BC Cicero goes to Greece for further
study.

78 BC Sulla dies.

77 BC Cicero returns to Rome. He mar-   *Pro Roscio Comoedo*
ries Terentia.

76 BC Tullia is born.

75 BC Cicero becomes quaestor. He is
appointed to Sicily.

70 BC Cicero successfully prosecutes   *In Verrem I*
Verres on behalf of the Sicilians.   *In Verrem II* (not spoken in court)
Verres flees the country.   *In Caecilium*

69 BC Cicero becomes aedile.   *Pro Fonteio*
                                                  Pro Caecina

67 BC Pompey wages a successful war
against the pirates.

66 BC Cicero becomes praetor. Manilian   *Pro Cluentio*
Law passed after Cicero speaks for it.   *De imperio Cn. Pompei (de lege Manilia)*

65 BC Cicero's son Marcus is born. The
first conspiracy of Catiline is formed.

64 BC Tullia is married to C. Piso.

63 BC Cicero becomes consul. The   *Pro Murena*
second conspiracy of Catiline is sup-   *In Catilinam I–IV*
pressed. Octavian (Augustus) is born.   *Pro Rabirio perduellionis reo*
                                                  De lege agraria contra Rullum I–III

62 BC Clodius violates Bona Dea. Cicero   *De Consulatu Suo* (poem)
testifies against him.   *Pro Sulla*
                                                  Pro Archia

61 BC Pompey celebrates his triumph
over Mithradates.

60 BC The first triumvirate is formed:
Caesar, Pompey, Crassus.

59 BC Caesar is consul. Clodius adopted by a plebeian and elected tribune.

Pro Flacco

58 BC Cicero exiled; Caesar goes to Gaul.

57 BC Cicero is recalled from exile.

Post reditum ad Quirites
Post reditum in Senatu
De domo sua
De haruspicum responso

56 BC Tullia, now a widow, is married to Furius Crassipes.

De provinciis consularibus
In Pisonem
In Vatinium
Pro Balbo
Pro Caelio
Pro Sestio
De Oratore: three books on oratory written as dialogue between two great orators—L. Crassus and M. Antonius.
De Legibus: a discussion of the nature of law.
De Re Publica: an examination of the various forms of government.

54 BC

Pro Scauro
Partitiones Oratoriae: a catechism on rhetoric.

53 BC Crassus is defeated and killed by the Parthians; Cicero is elected augur.

52 BC Clodius is killed by Milo.

Pro Milone

51 BC Cicero becomes proconsul of Cilicia.

50 BC Cicero returns to Rome; Tullia, now divorced, is married to Publius Cornelius Dolabella.

49 BC Caesar crosses the Rubicon in defiance of the Senate; Civil War begins. After much hesitation, Cicero sides with Pompey.

48 BC Caesar defeats Pompey. Pompey is murdered.

47 BC Caesar pardons Cicero, who returns to Rome, but has decreased political activity. Most of his speeches are pleas for exiled Pompeians.

46 BC Caesar is made dictator for ten

years. Cicero divorces Terentia and
marries Publilia. He begins a series of
philosophic writings.

45 BC Tullia dies after bearing a son,
who also dies. Cicero is devastated by
grief, divorces Publilia, and withdraws
into his writing.

44 BC Caesar is made dictator for life.
In March of this year, Caesar is as-
sassinated. Octavian comes to Rome.
Cicero delivers the Philippics I-IV.

43 BC Cicero writes Philippics V–XIV.
Octavian goes to war against Antony,
but through Lepidus the second
triumvirate is formed: Octavian,
Antony, Lepidus. Cicero meets death
at the hands of Antony's soldiers.

Pro Marcello
Brutus or *De Claris Oratoribus:* a history
of Roman oratory *(*46–44 BC)
Orator ad M. Brutum: description of the
ideal orator. (46–44 BC)
Paradoxa: explains Stoic philosophy.

Pro Ligario
Pro Rege Deiotaro
Tusculanae Disputationes: a discussion
of essentials for human happiness.
Academica: theories of philosophy.
De Finibus Bonorum et Malorum: Greek
ideas of good and evil.

De Optimo Genere Oratorum: an
introduction to a translation of
the speeches of Demosthenes and
Aeschines.
Topica ad C. Trebalium: an explanation
of Aristotle's *Topics,* for the use of
orators.
De Natura Deorum: an examination of
moral and theological problems and
of various philosophies.
Cato Maior or *De Senectute:* an essay in
praise of old age.
Laelius or *De Amicitia:* an essay on
friendship.
De Divinatione: a work dealing with
divine revelation and its perception by
mankind.
De Fato: Of Fate and Free Will; Cicero's
last treatise on religion.
De Officiis: a treatise setting forth the
moral views of a practical politician.

Philippicae I–XIV (44 to mid-43 BC)